Contents

Comet and Reverse Ajax: The Next-Generation Ajax 2.0

by Dave Crane and Phil McCarthy

This is a small book about a big subject.

As a technology, Ajax was small enough to be described in a few sentences, but it catalyzed huge changes in how we use web technologies (and communities, and business models). The full ramifications of those changes are still unfolding.

And in the middle of this change and upheaval, along comes Comet. Comet, simply put, allows you to send information from the server to the browser without the browser having to ask for it first. That's it—simple and itself very catalytic! Comet is still in its early days, but we believe that it's going to have a big impact on the way the Web unfolds over the next few years.

We're lucky enough to have our names on the front of this book, in exchange for which we spent the prescribed number of late nights in our lonely garrets, putting electronic pen to paper. However, a host of talented people behind us have made this possible. We'd like to extend our thanks to Tom Welsh, Richard Dal Porto, and Heather Lang of Apress for keeping us on schedule (and being patient when we weren't!) and for turning our rough drafts into flowing prose. We'd also like to thank Joe Walker of the DWR project, Greg Wilkins of the Jetty Web Server project, and Dylan Schiemann of the Dojo toolkit for answering our questions and for being generally supportive of our efforts to write this book— and, of course, for their broader support of the Ajax and Comet communities and turning out such interesting Open Source code in the first place.

Our friends, families, colleagues, and household pets have also been extremely patient and understanding, and we'd like to thank everyone in the Crane and McCarthy households, at Historic Futures, and Skillsmatter for their support.

Chapter 1: What Are Comet and Reverse Ajax?

The term "Comet" was coined by Alex Russell of the Dojo project to describe exchanges between a client and a server in which the server, rather than the client, initiates the contact. Joe Walker of the Direct Web Remoting (DWR) project refers to a similar mechanism as "Reverse Ajax." Much like when the term "Ajax" was coined in 2005, the name "Comet" has served as a rallying point around a number of previously disconnected technological projects, such as the nonblocking I/O introduced into Java in 2002, message queue technologies, and, further back, HTTP 1.1's persistent connections and the push technologies of the late 1990s.

These technologies have in common an interest in initiating communication between a client and a server from the server's end. Conventional web-based applications are all about client-led communication, but there has been a repeated need to discuss server-led communication within the web development community and to provide a name for it. To understand the phenomenon of Comet and Reverse Ajax, we need to consider why there is a need for it and why it is so out of the ordinary as to require a label of its own.

In this short book, you're going to address two tasks. You're going to learn the techniques being used to deliver Comet and Reverse Ajax in today's cutting-edge web toolkits. You're also going to cut your way through the various tangled incarnations of Comet, Reverse Ajax, and push to figure out why developers persist in trying to turn the HTTP request-response sequence on its head. What business need is there that only Comet (a.k.a. Reverse Ajax) can deliver? And is Comet always the best way to meet these needs?

WHAT IS AJAX?

We're assuming that you've heard the term "Ajax" before, but for those in need of a pithy, twenty-second, concise definition, here goes.

In most web applications, the client sends a request to the server only when refreshing the entire page, that is, all of the visual real estate that the user is looking at. "Ajax" refers to the ability to programmatically talk to the server in the background, without triggering a full-screen refresh.

Ajax may not sound like a big deal, but it's had big implications for the design of web applications, their workflow and usability, and even their business models. We are interested in Comet partly because we believe that it will have a similarly catalytic effect on the evolution of web-based technologies.

The Trouble with HTTP

To understand Comet, first you need to understand HTTP. As web developers, we're all somewhat familiar with HTTP—mostly as a part of the infrastructure that we take for granted and generally don't need to pay much attention to. Let's stop to give it our full attention for a moment.

HTTP was designed as a protocol for retrieving documents from remote servers, as illustrated in Figure 1-1. As such, it has two important characteristics:

- Communication between the client and the server is always initiated by the client and never by the server.

- Connections between the client and server are transient, and the server does not maintain any long-term state information regarding the client.

At least, this was the state of play with version 1.0 of the HTTP specification. By version 1.1, more application-like features, such as conversational state and persistent connections, were being talked about. We'll get to those shortly.

Figure 1-1. In a conventional HTTP request and response, the client initiates the communication.

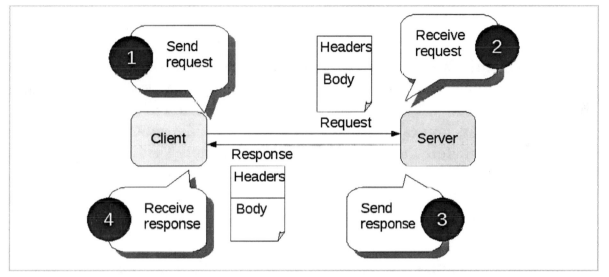

Comet challenges that first assumption and allows the server to decide when it should contact the client, as illustrated in Figure 1-2. According to the ground rules of HTTP then, Comet is already kicking up a storm.

Figure 1-2. In a Comet or Reverse Ajax exchange communication is initiated by the server.

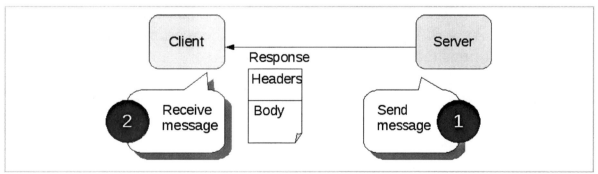

Figure 1-2 illustrates a single Comet exchange between server and client. Unlike the classic HTTP exchange depicted in Figure 1-1, the communication is only one-way, and it starts at the server. This is analogous to Steps 3 and 4 in Figure 1-1. Typically, the client won't respond to the server as part of this exchange, although within the larger life cycle of the application, the client will probably also talk to the server by initiating conventional HTTP requests.

Although Comet doesn't agree with HTTP, a number of workarounds can be used to implement Comet. In fact, we shouldn't really be bothered about breaking the ground rules of HTTP at all. If you look at the second rule stated previously, you can see that that is challenged by another common piece of infrastructure that we take for granted, namely the HTTP session. HTTP was never designed to preserve conversational state on the server, and in fact, the continuity of a session is ensured by the client (by passing a header or cookie to the server every time it makes a request to remind the server who it is).

At the time of its introduction, the HTTP session was seen as a clever hack of the HTTP model and as a catalyst that opened up many new use cases for the web, spawning the first generation of web applications. The concept of HTTP sessions is now well supported by all but the simplest of web servers and by all major web programming tools. Perhaps in time, Comet will become a standard part of the infrastructure that we can take for granted too. As you'll see in Chapters 6 and 7, work is already underway in reengineering web servers to better support Comet. For now, though, know that Reverse Ajax will suffice, so let's consider the reasons why you want to make use of this technique.

Some Common Use Cases

Let's assume for now that Comet can be made to work. Before starting to look at the technical details, we should perhaps ask why you're considering Comet at all. As you'll see in Chapter 2, there are several technical ways to address the problem, and you need to understand the nature of the problem correctly in order to pick the most suitable solution. Why, then, should you want the server to be able to contact the client? There are, in fact, several common use cases, so let's look at each one in turn.

Monitoring and Data Feeds

Most applications are designed to let the user actively engage with a domain model, for instance, by querying and updating it. On a desktop PC, applications that interact with the domain model include word processors, spreadsheets, file system browsers, and most of the functionality of e-mail clients. On the web, we include e-commerce applications and search engines in this category.

However, in a smaller but important class of application, the domain model is active, and the client takes on the role of a dashboard or monitor. E-mail clients function this way when they automatically check for new mail, as do utilities such as battery monitors. Within vertical industries, there is often strong demand for monitoring applications of this type, including applications to monitor specialized hardware in science/engineering and security applications, and stock ticker and other market data feeds in the financial arena. Message queue technologies, a standard part of the enterprise developer's toolkit, have been developed around these types of applications.

If we were to sketch the communication pattern between client and server for such an application, we might come up with something very similar to Figure 1-2.

Progress Updates

A second category in which Comet has a useful role to play is communicating progress on long-running server-side activities. In most web applications, contact with the server initiates server-side activity that is relatively brief, typically the execution of some business logic followed by a commit of the results to a database. In these cases, it is reasonable to make the user wait until the activity is completed before offering any feedback.

In some situations, however, contacting the server will initiate a longer running process. In this case, the process is best executed in a different thread, as illustrated in Figure 1-3. In this case, the user ought to be kept up to date as the long-running process unfolds, and the server may need to send several messages up to the client, possibly stating what percentage of the task is complete or listing key milestones.

Figure 1-3: Using Comet to report progress on a long-running server task

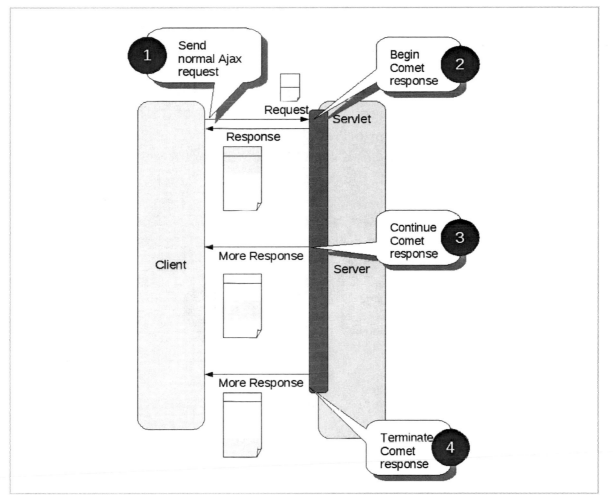

When reporting progress on a long-running server-side task, the connection may be kept open while the task executes, with response data being drip-fed to the client as significant milestones are reached.

Chat and Collaboration

In the applications that we have described so far, a single user has sole access to the domain model. While this is still true of the majority of desktop applications, on the web, multiple users frequently share a larger domain model (e.g., e-commerce and photo-sharing sites and chat systems). In these types of applications, the majority of traffic between client and server is still client-driven, but situations will arise in which one user has modified the shared model in such a way that it will affect other users' views of the model, as illustrated in Figure 1-4.

Figure 1-4: Mixing conventional Ajax and Reverse Ajax in a collaborative application

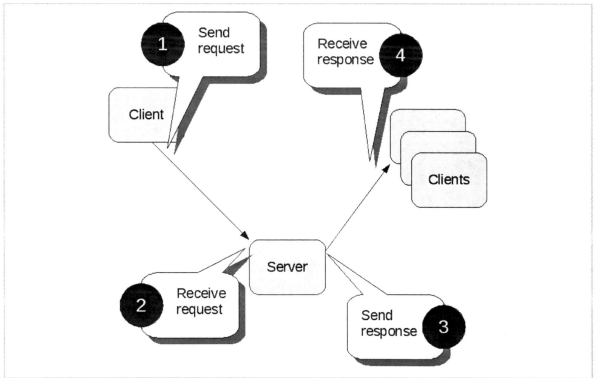

The sequence of events in this situation combines conventional Ajax HTTP calls with reverse Ajax. When one user submits an update, in a client-initiated exchange, the server may decide that other clients need to receive that update immediately. Reverse Ajax is then used to communicate these updates.

You don't always need Comet to deal with this situation. If the urgency of communicating the changes to the other users is low, you can simply wait for them to refresh their views and issue a warning if they try to commit updates that are no longer appropriate. Alternately, you may elect to notify them by an alternate route, such as sending e-mail.

These approaches may work for photo-sharing sites, for example, in which the timing of receiving an update is not critical. However, in other collaborative applications, for example, live chat systems and auctions, the entire workflow depends on instantaneous updates, so Comet has a significant role to play.

Summary

We've outlined three common scenarios in web application development in which we perceive a need for Comet. In the next chapter, you'll look at ways of implementing Comet and see how they fit the requirements that we've outlined here.

Chapter 2: Simple Ways to Achieve Push

In Chapter 1, we identified three common use cases that could benefit from using Comet. In this chapter, we'll cover some simple techniques that might address these use cases, without having to resort to Comet. In Chapter 3, you'll move on to look at simple implementations of Comet itself. If you want to really understand Comet, then you'll need to evaluate the alternatives and recognize the situations in which Comet is the best solution.

The Magnetic Poetry Application

As you're starting to delve into the nitty-gritty aspects of coding at this point, an example application would be useful. The application that you'll work with in this section (and through much of this book) is an online version of a magnetic 'fridge poetry set, in which words can be placed onto a surface and rearranged to make (hopefully) humorous or insightful phrases.

To add a Web 2.0–style twist to our application, we've decided to share the workspace among all users who are logged on. In terms of the use cases described in the "Common Use Cases" section of Chapter 1, you're creating a collaborative application in which multiple users will be manipulating a shared domain model at the same time.

You'll see the implementation details of our application in more detail as we proceed. For now, Figure 2-1 presents a screenshot of the application.

Figure 2-1. User interface of the magnetic poetry application

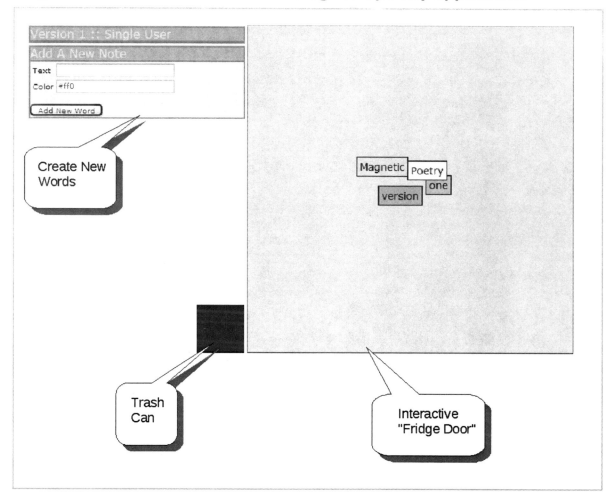

The UI of the application is fairly simple. The shared workspace on which the words appear occupies the majority of the screen space. The box on the left provides a drop-down form that allows users to add new words to the workspace and specify the text and the color. When first created, each word will be placed randomly on the workspace. Users position words (those they create themselves or those created by others—there's no permissions system!) using drag and drop. Finally, users can remove words from the workspace by dragging them into the trash can, which is situated near the bottom-left corner of the virtual refrigerator.

To implement the application in a single-user form (i.e., ignoring issues of collaboration for the moment), you need to provide Ajax callbacks for the basic CRUD methods–creating, reading, updating, and deleting elements. You'll make use of these in the following order:

1. When you first load the application, you'll make a call to the server to *read* the contents of the workspace (at this stage, reading could just as easily happen while loading the page, but we've made it a separate Ajax call because we know you'll need it to be that way as soon as you introduce collaboration).

2. When the user adds a new word to the workspace, you'll make an Ajax call to create the entity on the server-side domain model.

3. When the user moves a word, you'll update the coordinates in the domain model.

4. When the user drags a word into the trash can, you'll delete it from the domain model.

We've implemented the server side using Groovy on Grails, simply because that system is very well suited to quickly setting up this sort of application. On the client side, you'll be using the Prototype and Scriptaculous libraries to implement the application to make easy work of creating the drag-and-drop features. We've chosen to send data between the client and server using the JavaScript Object Notation (JSON) format, because Grails and Prototype both support it very well and because it is simple to use. We also cheated and read the rest of this book first, so we know that the Comet community is standardizing on JSON for the Bayeux protocol, which we discuss in Chapters 6 and 7.

WHAT ARE ALL THESE BUZZWORDS?

We've done rather a lot of name-dropping in the last paragraph or two. For those of you not familiar with the various technologies that we're using to build our examples, here's a very quick rundown.

Groovy is a scripting language built on top of Java, that interoperates very well with Java but can be more flexible and concise. For more information, visit `http://groovy.codehaus.org`.

Grails is a full-featured Model-View-Controller web framework built using Groovy. We've chosen Grails for this book because it automates all the standard web application features that we don't want to focus on, leaving us more time to talk about Comet. Find out more about Grails at `http://grails.org`.

Prototype and *Scriptaculous* are popular JavaScript libraries for web development and Ajax applications. Prototype is a general-purpose utility library, and Scriptaculous provides user-interface capabilities such as animation and drag-and-drop functionality. Their home pages are `http://prototypejs.org` and `http://script.aculo.us` (clever, huh?).

JavaScript Object Notation (JSON) is a compact serialization format for objects that is supported natively by JavaScript. JSON has also become a very popular way to transfer data between the browser and server in Ajax applications. Prototype and Grails both provide a number of features that make using JSON very easy. The site `http://json.org` is dedicated to discussing JSON.

We won't run through the entire codebase of the Magnetic Poetry application in detail here; you'll just cover the basic CRUD methods. The full source code is available from the Source Code/Download link on the Apress web site, and we want to get back to the topic at hand in pretty short order.

Creating New Words

The user of the application can create a new word simply by filling in the form and submitting it. You're intercepting the form programmatically and making an Ajax call to the server, as follows:

```
function addWord(){
   var text=$F('word_text');
   var color=$F('word_color');
   var x=Math.floor(Math.random()*350);
   var y=Math.floor(Math.random()*420);
   var paramsObj={ text:text, color:color, x:x, y:y };
   ncw Ajax.Request(
     "simple/create",
     { parameters: paramsObj,
       evalJSON:"force",
       onSuccess:function(response){
         new Word(response.responseJSON.created);
       }
     }
   );
}
```

Reading Words

As we noted in our discussion of Figure 2-1, the user supplies the text and color for the word, and the word's initial position is randomly allocated by the client. The server will return a JSON expression that evaluates to an object that contains the full set of data for our new word, including the database ID. You can use this to define a client-side Word object that then renders itself onscreen using Prototype's DOM helper and string interpolation methods. Here are the constructor and the render() method of the Word object:

```
var Word=Class.create({
  initialize:function(props){
    Object.extend(this,props);
    Words["_"+this.id]=this;
    this.render();
  },
  render:function(){
    var tmpl="<div id='note_#{id}' class='note' "
      +"style='top:#{y}px;left:#{x}px;"
      +"background-color:#{color}'>"
      +"#{text}</div>";
    var html=tmpl.interpolate(this)
    $("board").insert({top:html});
    this.body=$("note_"+this.id);
    this.body.word=this;
    new Draggable(this.body);
  }
}
```

Note that you don't create the client-side object until the server has responded, so that you can assign the ID of the object. You'll need that ID when you update or delete the object later.

You can use a similar JSON format when the application initializes to read the set of words stored in the database. The callback function from this Ajax call is similar, except that you need to iterate through an array of result items. Here's the implementation of the getWords() function:

```
function getWords(){
  new Ajax.Request(
    "simple/read",
    { evalJSON: "force",
      onComplete:function(response){
        var results=response.responseJSON.results;
        results.each(
          function(result){ new Word(result); }
        );
```

```
      }
    }
  );
}
```

Updating Words

Now that you've sorted out the "C" and "R" of CRUD, you need to
implement update and delete functionality. You can add these as methods
of the Word object rather than top-level functions. When the user moves a
word, you call Word.update():

```
update:function(dx,dy){
  this.x=parseInt(this.x)+dx;
  this.y=parseInt(this.y)+dy;
  var params={
    id: this.id,
    x: this.x,
    y: this.y
  };
  new Ajax.Request(
    "simple/update",
    { parameters: params,
      evalJSON: "force",
      onSuccess:function(response){
        var updated=response.responseJSON.updated;
      }.bind(this)
    }
  );
},
```

In this implementation, update() is essentially a fire-and-forget method.
The response lists a few properties of the updated item, but you have no
real need to read them at this point.

Deleting Words

Your implementation of delete is similar. The function is called
deleteMe(), because "delete" is a reserved word in Internet Explorer's
JScript. You can also treat deleteMe() as a fire-and-forget method for
now and not worry about parsing the server response:

```
deleteMe:function(){
  this.pendingDeletion=true;
  new Ajax.Request(
    "simple/delete",
    { parameters: { id: this.id },
      evalJSON: "force",
      onSuccess: function(response){
        var deleted=response.responseJSON.deleted;
        if (deleted.id==this.id){
          this.body.style.zIndex=3;
          new Effect.Puff(this.body);
          Words["_"+this.attr.id]=null;
        }
      }.bind(this)
    }
  );
}
```

You've now created the basic CRUD functionality for your application, but
it's a single-user application, and composing magnetic poetry on the
refrigerator door only really becomes fun when your family or housemates
join in. To support a shared workspace in which several users can add
words simultaneously, you'll need to introduce some form of push into our
application. In the next section, you'll see how to modify the application to
do that.

Introducing Push Using Polling

Ideally, you want several users to be able to log in to our application at once. When one user adds a new word, moves a word, or drags a word to the trash can, you want every client to be updated. In terms of the use cases for push that we described in Chapter 1, you're effectively describing a collaborative application.

The simplest way to implement this collaborative ability is by polling the server, as illustrated in Figure 2-2. The client makes a regular request to the server asking for updates, and the server responds- -often simply reporting that there's nothing to report. Polling tends to be wasteful of network and server resources, but it's an easy place to start, so let's see how you get on with it.

Figure 2-2. In simple polling, the client repeatedly contacts the server to check for changes in the domain model. Updates initiated by the user do not affect the polling schedule.

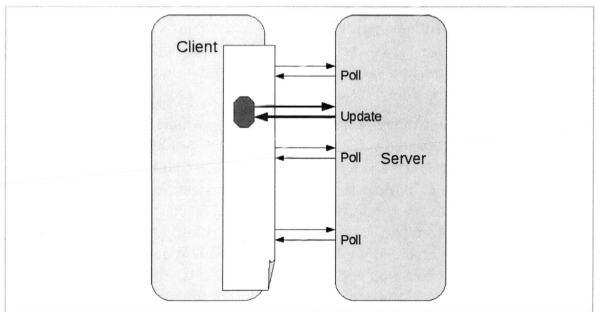

First, you need to handle the business of setting up the repeated requests to the server. You can do this using JavaScript's built-in timeout mechanism, as illustrated in the following code:

```
var poll={
  timer:null,
  interval:3,
  run:function(){
    this.stop();
    this.timer=setTimeout(
      function(){ getWords(); }.bind(this),
      this.interval*1000
    );
  },
  stop:function(){
    if (this.timer){
      clearTimeout(this.timer);
    }
  }
};
```

Here, you define a little helper with two methods: `run()` and `stop()`. When you invoke `run()`, you set up a timer that will call the `getWords()` function in the future, and you take a reference to the timer, so that you can clear it by calling the `stop()` method.

JavaScript has a built-in method `setInterval()`, which can be used to invoke a function repeatedly. That sounds ideal for a polling interval, so why haven't you used it? The answer lies in the fact that the network is inherently unreliable. In order for your updates to be received in a timely fashion, you want to set a short polling interval, a few seconds at most. If network conditions are bad, it might take an equivalent time to receive a response from the server, so you'd be firing multiple requests simultaneously. Instead, you will fire a new request when you receive the response from the previous one. Hence, modify the read method as follows:

```
function getWords(){
  var versions=$H(Words).collect(
    function(pair){
      var word=pair.value;
      return word.id+"="+word.version;
    }
  ).join(" ");
  new Ajax.Request(
    "poll/read",
    { evalJSON: "force",
      parameters: { "versions": versions },
      onComplete:function(response){
        var results=response.responseJSON.results;
        results.each(
          function(result){
            if (Words["_"+result.id]){
              var word=Words["_"+result.id];
              if (result.deleted){
                word.deleteUI();
              }else{
                word.updateUI(result.x,result.y,
                  result.version);
              }
            }else{
              new Word(result);
            }
          }
        );
        poll.run();
      }
    }
  );
}
```

Note that you call `poll.run()` in the callback function that you pass to the `Ajax.Request()` when you create it.

This function also introduces the change that you need to make to your domain model and to the data you send in the request and response. When you ask the server for updates, it needs to know how much you already know. In a very naive implementation, you could send all the information about every word on the board whenever you respond and let the client figure out what had changed. In such a setup, most of the data would be redundant. You can tighten up the exchange of information in one of two ways:

- Assign a version number to each entity, and increment it when you update. If the client tells the server the current version of each element it knows about, the server can compare version numbers and send only entities for which a newer version exists.

- Assign a last-updated timestamp to each entity, and send the time of the last update with each request for updates. The server can then send data for entities updated since the client last called.

Both approaches fulfill your basic requirements of ensuring data integrity and managing concurrency. We've opted to use the version number approach here, partly because the domain objects created by Grails are automatically assigned a version number that gets updated for you whenever the underlying data is changed. If you were to code either solution from scratch, you'd need to manually manage the version or timestamp fields. By leveraging Grails existing version numbers, you simply need to assemble a lookup object and send it to the server as an additional parameter when we make a read request.

When the response comes back, you can no longer simply create a new word for each entry. If you already have a word with a matching ID, you will update it instead, by calling the update() method, which now accepts a version number too. Further, you may have passed down a version number for a word that no longer exists, if another user has deleted it from the system. In this case, the server will return a JSON object with two properties, the ID and a property `deleted` set to `true`.

To accommodate these updates, you've pulled the UI-updating code in your `Word` object out into separate methods: `deleteUI()` and `updateUI()`. The implementation for the `Word` object now looks like this:

```
var Word=Class.create({
  initialize:function(props){ /* no change*/ },
  render:function(){ /* no change */ },
  update:function(dx,dy){
    this.x=parseInt(this.x)+dx;
    this.y=parseInt(this.y)+dy;
    var params={
      id: this.id,
      x: this.x,
      y: this.y
    };
    new Ajax.Request(
      "poll/update",
      { parameters: params,
        evalJSON: "force",
        onSuccess:function(response){
          var updated=response.responseJSON.updated;
        }.bind(this)
      }
    );
  },
  updateUI:function(x,y,version){
    this.x=x;
    this.y=y;
    if (version){ this.version=version; }
    this.body.setStyle({
      "left":x+"px","top":y+"px"
    });
  },
```

```
deleteMe:function(){
  this.pendingDeletion=true;
  new Ajax.Request(
    "poll/delete",
    { parameters: { id: this.id },
      evalJSON: "force",
      onSuccess: function(response){
        var deleted=response.responseJSON.deleted;
        if (deleted.id==this.id){
          this.deleteUI();
        }
      }.bind(this)
    }
  );
},
deleteUI:function(){
  this.body.style.zIndex=3;
  new Effect.Puff(this.body);
  Words["_"+this.attr.id]=null;
}
});
```

The update() method is still fire-and-forget. A word that has been moved is already visually up to date, before you even contact the server. In the case of the deleteMe() call, though, you update the UI when the server returns a response and use the same deleteUI() call that the getWords() method uses when it receives notification that another user has dragged a word to the trash can.

You've now got a working collaborative application. If you set the poll interval low enough, the responsiveness of the application is good enough to count as a live update of the other users' activities. Unfortunately, setting a short poll interval also results in heavier network and server load. Any polling solution faces this trade-off between responsiveness and overuse of resources.

Improving Efficiency Using Piggybacking

A polling strategy faces a stark trade-off between heavy use of resources and poor response time. You can improve the situation to some extent if you consider that you're not currently making much use of the response when you perform an update or delete action. If you send the version information with all calls to the server and expect updates in the response, you can cut down on the number of requests made purely to poll the server.

This technique is often referred to as piggybacking data, as the contents of the response aren't strictly related to the nature of the request but are being carried along with it anyway. Figure 2-3 illustrates piggybacking at work. We'll conclude this chapter by looking at how we'd implement this approach.

Figure 2-3. In piggybacking, responses to updates initiated by the user will also contain any changes to the domain model and will reset the polling schedule.

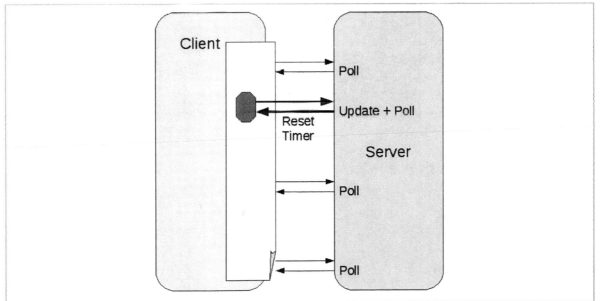

First, you're going to break out the code that generates the version numbers on the client into a separate method:

```
var getVersions=function(){
  return $H(Words).collect(
    function(pair){
      var word=pair.value;
      return word.id+"="+word.version;
    }
  ).join(" ");
}
```

Second, you'll define a common Ajax callback function, so that all your responses will have the same format whether you're reading, creating, updating, or deleting:

```
var callback=function(response){
  var results=response.responseJSON.results;
  results.each(
    function(result){
      if (Words["_"+result.id]){
        var word=Words["_"+result.id];
        if (result.deleted){
          word.deleteUI();
        }else{
          word.updateUI(result.x,result.y,
            result.version);
        }
      }else{
        new Word(result);
      }
    }
  );
  poll.run();
}
```

You're still triggering the next call to the polling mechanism when the response comes in. When you create, update, or delete, you need to do three things:

- Stop the polling thread, because you're going to receive an update from the current request. You'll restart it again when you receive the response.

- Gather information on current versions, and add it as an extra request parameter

- Pass the common callback function to the request object

The read method now looks like this:

```
function getWords(){
  poll.stop();
  new Ajax.Request(
    "piggy/read",
    { evalJSON: "force",
      parameters: { "versions": getVersions() },
      onComplete: callback
    }
  );
}
```

Your create method has a similarly-formed Ajax request now too:

```
function addWord(){
  poll.stop();
  var text=$F('word_text');
  var color=$F('word_color');
  var x=Math.floor(Math.random()*350);
  var y=Math.floor(Math.random()*420);
  var paramsObj={ text:text, color:color,
    x:x, y:y, versions: getVersions() };
```

```
new Ajax.Request(
  "piggy/create",
  { parameters: paramsObj,
    evalJSON:"force",
    onSuccess:callback
  }
);
}
```

And the update method does too:

```
update:function(dx,dy){
  poll.stop();
  this.x=parseInt(this.x)+dx;
  this.y=parseInt(this.y)+dy;
  var params={
    id: this.id,
    x: this.x,
    y: this.y,
    versions: getVersions()
  };
  new Ajax.Request(
    "piggy/update",
    { parameters: params,
      evalJSON: "force",
      onSuccess:callback
    }
  );
},
```

And, finally, here's the delete method:

```
deleteMe:function(){
  poll.stop();
  this.pendingDeletion=true;
  new Ajax.Request(
    "piggy/delete",
    { parameters: { id: this.id,
      versions:getVersions() },
```

```
        evalJSON: "force",
        onSuccess: callback
      }
    );
  },
```

You've tidied your code up quite a bit in the process and made better use of
the network, particularly if the users are busily engaged in modifying the
board. On the server side, you need to modify your code in a similar way:
break out a generic method to compute the updates and have every server-
side method ultimately call that method. To illustrate this, let's look at the
difference between the delete method for the polling and the piggybacking
solutions.

In the simple polling example, you delete the entity and render a JSON
response directly:

```
def delete = {
  def id=params['id']
  def word=Word.get(id)
  word.delete()
  render(contentType:"text/json"){
    deleted(
      id:word.id,
    )
  }
}
```

The JSON is generated by the call to render(). The closures within the
render() call will generate a nested data structure. If you're not familiar
with Groovy's Builder objects, just take our word for it for now that the
preceding code works. More information about Groovy Builders can be
found at http://groovy.codehaus.org/Builders.

When you move to the piggybacking solution, the read() method
generates a comprehensive update, so you just invoke that:

```
def delete - {
  def id=params['id']
  def word=Word.get(id)
  word.delete()
  read()
}
```

The generic update will automatically include the element that you've deleted, just as if it had been deleted by another user, so you don't need to worry about adding any custom response to cover that.

Summary

You've now taken your collaborative application about as far as you can using traditional Ajax requests and responses. In the next chapter, we'll start to address Comet proper and see what it has to offer; but for now, let's review how far we've come.

The simplest approach to pushing data from the server was to poll the server repeatedly. While this approach works, it places a heavy load on available resources of both the server itself and the network. Every connected client is continually transmitting data—usually to be told by the server that nothing has changed—and the server must handle each of these connections. You can lighten the load by increasing the interval between polls, but that decreases the system's responsiveness to updates, which is often one of the fundamental requirements of a collaborative application.

Piggybacking provides a partial salve to these problems but will only really help in situations where the user frequently sends updates to the server anyway. In the case of passive monitoring of the server-side data model, we see no gain.

The results so far can, at best, be described as satisfactory, but certainly not exciting. Looking at the other side of the equation, we need to consider how much effort we have expended to provide this minimal amount of push. One simple metric is file size. Compared with the noncollaborative codebase, the piggybacking code contains roughly 25 percent more JavaScript, and the increase in size of the controller code on the server side is similar. You're adding a lot of additional plumbing code by hand to manage the push-based updates of your model.

Wouldn't it be nice if some of that additional code could be omitted? To that end, you'll continue rolling your own code in the next section and take your first steps towards using Comet.

Chapter 3: Introducing Comet

In Chapter 2, you looked at polling and piggybacking techniques to see how far you could get with creating an interactive collaborative application. Along the way, you found yourself juggling timeout periods, responsiveness, and server/network loads, without reaching a satisfactory balance between the various factors.

Using Comet techniques, you can simplify matters. In this section, you're going to look at the basic building blocks of Comet and implement those building blocks from scratch yourself within a standard web application framework (Groovy on Grails). Along the way, you'll see how Comet can improve your applications' responsiveness, and you'll discover a whole new set of issues. The examples that we present here are designed to illustrate the issues surrounding Comet.

In this chapter, you'll be replacing your polling/piggybacking mechanism with Comet and using it to update your domain model on the fly. First, though, we're going to introduce a somewhat simpler feature that will allow you to come to grips with coding Comet on the client.

Later, in Chapters 4 through 7, we'll look at a couple of best of breed implementations—the dedicated support for Comet offered by DWR and Cometd/Bayeux.

Implementing a Comet Feed Using XHR

Recall that in a normal HTTP call to the server, the response is completed very soon after the arrival of the request, and the arrival of the response can generally be treated as a single event on the client side. With Comet, we keep the response stream open for a significantly longer time and typically send several pieces of data back in the response, each of which is treated as a discrete event on the client. Figure 3-1 illustrates the process.

Figure 3-1. The Comet request is held open on the server for a while, during which time multiple discrete changes are communicated back to the client.

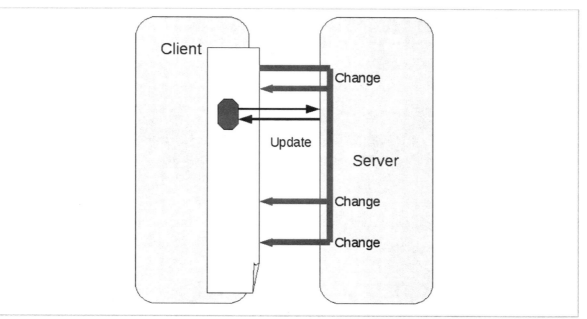

In Chapter 1, we identified several use cases for Comet. Throughout Chapter 2, we focused on the collaborative application, arguably the most complex of the lot. We also identified Comet as being well suited to long-running server-side processes, and in the latest version of our application, you'll introduce just such a feature.

Assume the Magnetic Pottery service allows the user of our interactive refrigerator door to order a custom set of real ceramic refrigerator magnets matching the online content of the application. Of course, firing up the kiln, shaping the clay, and baking all the items can't be accomplished in a matter of milliseconds, so you'll want to keep the user informed as the various stages of the process occur.

To do this, you're going to set up a server-side process that won't release the response immediately but rather keep it open until the entire operation has completed, which could take several days! We know that you're busy people, though, so for the sake of the examples in this book, we've cut the baking down to 30 to 40 seconds, which is still an unusually long time for a web request.

How do you keep the request alive? The simplest approach is to put the servlet thread to sleep and continue processing when you wake it up. The implementation of our server-side code shows this process:

```
def bake={
    response.contentType='text/plain'
    def writer=response.getWriter()
    writeText(writer,"firing up the oven",2000)
    def words=Word.findAll()
    for (w in words){
        writeText(writer,
            "shaping clay for '"
            +w.text+"'",1000)
    }
    writeText(writer,"baking...",6000)
    writeText(writer,"still baking...",4000)
    writeText(writer,
        "tum de tum, nice day today?",3000)
    writeText(writer,"still baking...",6000)
    writeText(writer,"nearly done now",2000)
    writeText(writer,"there - baked!",1000)
    writeText(writer,"cooling...",2000)
    writeText(writer,"wrapping parcel",2000)
    writeText(writer,"sending to dispatch",2000)
}

def writeText(writer,text,sleeptime){
    writer.write(text+"\n");
    writer.flush()
    Thread.currentThread().sleep(sleeptime)
}
```

The entry point for the request is the method called `bake`. You prime the response by setting a MIME type and repeatedly call the `writeText()` method. `writeText()` takes three arguments. The first is a Java `Writer` object (i.e., a character-based output stream) belonging to the response object; anything written to this stream will end up in the HTTP response. The remaining two arguments are the text to write to the output stream and the amount of time to suspend the thread for after the text is written. In a richer example, you'd have a message bus connected to the kiln, delivering new inputs, but let's keep it simple for now.

In this implementation of `writeText()`, you need to do two unusual things. First, you explicitly `flush()` the stream after writing to it to ensure that the part of the response that you've just written actually crosses the network immediately, rather than being stored in a local buffer on the server. Second, you get a reference to and suspend the current thread. While the thread is suspended, the servlet cannot exit, and the response doesn't complete until after the last call to `writeText()` has returned.

Were you to watch the response, you would see several small pieces of text being returned to the client throughout its lifetime. Many of the common HTTP debugging tools, such as Firebug, won't actually show you this, as they update the display only when the request is completed (since you're using HTTP in an unusual way here, you can't expect all the tools and APIs that you encounter to be ideal for our purposes).

We come across similar issues, in fact, when you look at your client-side code. If you look at the design of the `XMLHttpRequest` object (`XHR` for short) that underpins most Ajax calls in web browsers, you'll see that it supports a number of ready states, representing the points in the life cycle of the request or response. Any callback function that you assign to the `XHR` object will be invoked when each of these ready states is reached. The ready states are defined in the following table.

READY STATE	DESCRIPTION
Uninitialized	The request hasn't been sent yet
Loading	The request is underway. We're awaiting a response.
Loaded	The response has started to come back.
Interactive	The response has come back sufficiently for us to begin reading it.
Complete	The response has completed.

The ready states provide a fairly complete description of the life cycle of a request and response, but unfortunately, they don't cover a prolonged response very evenly. The most interesting time is when you've received some data but are waiting for more data to come in. So you'll hit the interactive state fairly quickly, when the first message reaches the browser, and won't be notified again until the last message comes in. Actually, this is a worst-case scenario. In some browsers, you'll get notified more frequently, but you can't rely on that. Once you hit the interactive state, you'll need to set up your own timer to repeatedly check for new data. The JavaScript code required to update the user on the progress of his refrigerator magnet set follows:

```
var baker={
  localPollInterval:0.5,
  start:function(){
    this.output=$("bake_status");
    $("bake_button").hide();
    this.output.show();
    new Ajax.Request(
      "comet/bake",
      { method: "get",
        onInteractive:function(response){
          this.xhr=response.request.transport;
          this.listen();
        }.bind(this),
```

```
    onComplete:function(){
      this.done();
    }.bind(this)
  }
  );
},
listen:function(){
  if (this.timer){ clearTimeout(this.timer); }
  this.timer=setTimeout(
    function(){
      var text=this.xhr.responseText;
      var lines=text.split("\n");
      var latest=(lines.length>1)
        ? lines[lines.length-2]
        : "waiting for server";
      this.output.innerHTML=latest;
      this.listen();
    }.bind(this),
    this.localPollInterval*1000
  );
},
done:function(){
  if (this.timer){ clearTimeout(this.timer); }
  this.output.hide();
  $("bake_button").show();
}
}
```

The `baker` object has three methods representing the life cycle of the
Comet request. The `start()` method hides the button to prevent multiple
submits, identifies the output element on screen, and initiates the call to the
server. You're using Prototype's `Ajax.Request` object here. Idiomatic use
of `Ajax.Request` typically involves adding only one callback when the
request completes, but the object does accept callbacks corresponding to
any ready state. Here, you've added callbacks to both the interactive and
the complete stages.

When the request hits the interactive state, you call the `baker` object's `listen()` method. First, though, you get a reference from the `Ajax.Request` to the underlying XHR object. Again, you're encountering a mismatch between the expected use of HTTP and Comet. Prototype's Ajax classes construct an `Ajax.Response` object that they pass back as an argument to callback functions, decorated with a number of extra useful features. Normally, to read the response body, you simply look at the `response.responseText` property. However, this property is set when the interactive stage is first reached, and `response.responseText` won't update as further data comes in. To read the latest data, you need to bypass Prototype's abstractions and grab the underlying XHR object itself.

The `listen()` method sets up a timer and calls itself repeatedly, reading the XHR `responseText`. You're polling here, but only locally on the client, not across the network, so you can afford to set a much shorter polling interval. We've chosen half a second here, because you're displaying human-readable output. Anything shorter would be less than the average human reaction time!

The format of the data is quite simple in this case, with each message returned by the server being a single line of text. Whenever you read `XHR.responseText`, you get back the total response to date, not just the last message sent, so you need to do a bit of string manipulation to extract the last line.

The `onComplete()` callback to the `Ajax.Request` simply cancels the timer and tidies up the user interface, allowing the user to click the button again.

As this section illustrates, you can handle Comet using the standard XHR object that underpins most Ajax frameworks. Support for Comet is far from ideal, particularly in the way that we had to identify the latest piece of content to arrive. There are other mechanisms for receiving Comet feeds on the client, which we'll address briefly before we get back to Cometizing the main part of our application.

Script Tags, Iframes, and Comet

The fundamental problem with XHR and Comet is that XHR is designed around the notion that the response will return quickly and can be treated as a single event. We come across this assumption in many HTTP clients and within web browsers, but by a stroke of luck, one mechanism within the browser doesn't make this assumption. That is the humble `<script>` tag.

Whenever a web browser encounters a `<script>` tag, whether in the head or body of a document, it will execute the script immediately, without waiting for the rest of the document to load. This behavior is most familiar to web developers as a mild annoyance, requiring code to be wrapped in a callback to the `window.onload` event to prevent it from executing until DOM nodes are properly resolved. But it makes a first-rate transport for Comet.

If you were to port your progress report to using this technique, rather than setting up an XHR object, you would create a hidden `iframe` pointing at the server-side resource:

```
<iframe style='width:0px; height:0px'
    src='comet/bake'></iframe>
```

Set `size` to `0px` rather than setting `display:none`, because some browsers optimize the rendering of a nondisplaying iframe by not fetching its contents from the server.

You would also need to modify your server-side `writeText()` method as follows to emit `<script>` tags rather than plain text:

```
def writeText(writer,text,sleeptime){
  writer.write(
    "<script>top.baker.output(\""
    +text
    +"\")</script>\n"
  );
  writer.flush()
  Thread.currentThread().sleep(sleeptime)
}
```

Each script tag references the JavaScript `baker` object as `top.baker` and invokes an `output()` method on it defined as follows:

```
baker:function(msg){
  this.output.innerHTML=msg;
}
```

You'll continue to work with the XHR object in this chapter, but if you prefer a script-centric approach, iframes offer a useful transport mechanism for Comet.

Long Polling

You've taken your first steps with Comet now, but the core of our application is still running on a combination of piggybacking and old-fashioned polling. It's time to replace those features with a Comet-like technique. You're going to maintain an open request to the server at all times.

While running, this request will scan the domain model for changes, using the same version number technique as before and return only when it detects a change. You could leave the response open for further updates, potentially for several minutes or even hours, but assume you've elected to return on the first change. This is a variation on Comet often referred to as long polling, and it's illustrated in Figure 3-2. In traditional polling, the request is open only for a very short time during the polling interval, whereas in long polling the request is open almost continually.

Figure 3-2. In long polling, the request only returns one response but is made well ahead of time and kept open until something interesting happens on the server.

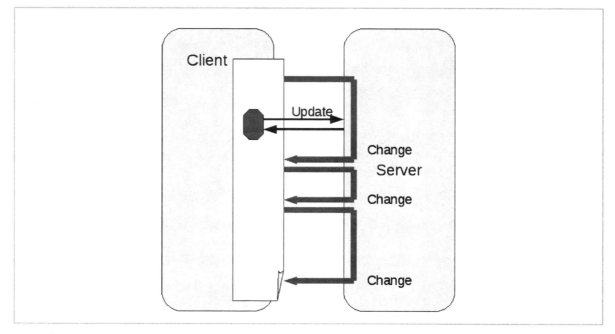

Let's take a look at the server-side code required to support long polling First, you've provided a couple of configuration parameters in the controller:

```
def tries=600
def blink=100
```

The variable `tries` specifies the maximum number of reads of the data model before returning. `blink` specifies the sleep time between reading the data model. So, your default setting is to keep the request open for a maximum of 60 seconds and poll (locally, on the server) the data model every 100 milliseconds. You'll make use of these parameters now in the read method that gets executed when you fire the request:

```
def read = {
  def writer=response.getWriter()
  def versions = [:]
  def knownVersions=params['versions']
  versions=[:]
  if (knownVersions!=null &&
      knownVersions.length()>0) {
    for (pair in knownVersions.split(" ")) {
      def bits=pair.split("=")
      versions[bits[0]]=Integer.parseInt(bits[1],10)
    }
  }
  response.contentType='text/json'
  def counter=0
  checkChanges: while (counter<tries) {
    def changes=getChanges(versions);
    if (changes.size()>0) {
      def content="{ 'tick':"+counter
        +", 'results':["+changes.join(", ")+"] }"
      render(content)
      break checkChanges
    }else{
      Thread.currentThread().sleep(blink)
      counter+=1
    }
  }
  if (counter>=tries) {
    render("{ 'tick':"+tries+", 'results':[] }");
  }
}
```

First, you unpack the latest known version numbers sent to us by the client, as before. You next enter a named `while` loop called `checkChanges`, which runs on a counter that will execute up to the maximum specified in the `tries` variable. Within this loop, you repeatedly hit a second method called getChanges() and sleep for the specified time if no changes are encountered. If you do encounter changes, you render some JSON data and exit the loop. Finally, if you've used up all your tries and encountered nothing, you render an empty result set and exit the loop.

What does the getChanges() method do? Let's look at the code:

```
def getChanges(versions){
  def words=Word.findAll()
  def knownIds=new ArrayList(versions.keySet())
  def entries=[]
  for (w in words){
    w.refresh()          ·
    def key=""+w.id
    def known=versions[key]
    knownIds.remove(key)
    def upToDate=(known!=null && known==w.version)
    if (!upToDate){
      entries.add("{'id':'"+w.id
        +"', 'version':'"+w.version
        +"', 'text':'"+w.text
        +"', 'color':'"+w.color
        +"', 'x':'"+w.x
        +"', 'y':'"+w.y
        +"'}"
      )
    }
  }
  knownIds.clone().each{ id ->
    entries.add("{'id':'"+id+"', 'deleted':true}")
  }
  return entries
}
```

You retrieve all the words in the data model using findAll(). You iterate through each word, refreshing it against the database and comparing it with the latest known version. If you encounter a newer version of a word, you build up some JSON code to capture the latest data. You also keep a list of words that you think you know about in the knownIds variable. You remove IDs from this list as you encounter them, so that you can flag any remaining IDs as no longer being in the database. You then return the list of JSON expressions that represents the updated or deleted changes.

Throughout this chapter, you've seen abstractions in framework code that make assumptions about HTTP that no longer hold true when you're using Comet. You've run into two more in the getChanges() method.

First, Grails follows a common practice in web frameworks of isolating a request within a database transaction. That is, between the start and end of the request, it will see no changes to the data model other than those it makes itself, and its own changes will be committed only at the end of the request. For short-lived requests, that provides a sensible layer of transaction demarcation, but for our long-polling technique or a continuous Comet feed, it could present a problem. With Comet, you are deliberately preventing the request from completing while polling for changes to the model that have occurred within the request's lifetime, and therefore within the current transaction. Fortunately, Grails's object-relational mapping (ORM) layer provides a refresh() method on the domain objects that allows us explicitly to request changes from the database, rather than using the cached values presented at the start of the request.

The second abstraction that you run up against is in the way Grails renders data. If you're an astute reader, you will have noticed that we indulged in some rather prehistoric behavior: assembling JSON data by hand using string concatenation, rather than using the Grails JSONBuilder to construct data programmatically, as you have done elsewhere. The reason for this is that the Grails render method helpfully flushes and closes the output stream for us after rendering the data. Normally, this is a nice touch, as it saves us from a little extra housekeeping, but in the case of Comet, you may want to flush without closing. We have chosen to write the data manually rather than refactoring the Grails renderers here.

Leaving these issues to the side, we have now covered everything that you need to retrieve updates from the server using Comet. You don't need to modify the read, update, or delete methods, because you'll continue to use ordinary Ajax to handle them. Let's take a look at the client-side code:

```
function getWords(){
  new Ajax.Request(
    "comet/read",
    { evalJSON: "force",
      parameters: { "versions": getVersions() },
      onComplete:function(response){
        var jsonObj=response.responseJSON;
        var results=jsonObj.results;
        results.each(
          function(result){
            if (Words["_"+result.id]){
              var word=Words["_"+result.id];
              if (result.deleted){
                word.deleteUI();
              }else{
                word.updateUI(result.x,result.y,
                  result.version);
              }
            }else{
              new Word(result);
            }
          }
        );
        poll.run();
      }
    }
  );
}
```

The client-side code required to implement long polling is actually quite minimal and should familiar from your early experiments with polling in Chapter 2. You need to respond only when the request has completed, and you need to parse the results as before. There's no need to catch the interactive status as you did for the Magnetic Poetry example, because the long poll will return only one piece of data.

The create, update, and delete methods of your Word object have reverted to using the PollController that we presented in Chapter 2, so you've now successfully implemented a Comet-based version of our Magnetic Poetry application, using both multipart Comet and long polling. Along the way, you've encountered a lot of interesting technical challenges, so let's wrap up by reviewing them.

Issues with Naive Comet Implementations

On the server-side, you came across several mismatches between the expectations of the web framework you were using and the way you're using HTTP to support Comet. Specifically, the database abstraction layer in Grails was based on the Session in View pattern (see http://www.hibernate.org/43.html for a very detailed discussion on Session in View). You had to take extra steps to see changes made to the database during the lifetime of the request. Second, Grails's rendering mechanism was at odds with keeping the output stream open after rendering structured data. Grails isn't doing anything out of the ordinary here, and you'd be likely to encounter similar issues in a number of popular web frameworks.

On the client side, you saw similar mismatches with the Prototype Javascript library's Ajax utility objects. Rather than handing back the raw XHR object, Prototype provides an artificially generated Response object, which contains a number of extra convenience methods not found in the native XHR object. The responseText property of this Ajax.Response object fails to keep up to date as more data arrives through the Comet transport, forcing us to cut through the abstraction to the raw XHR object beneath. This issue applies only when using Comet, not with the long polling approach.

In addition to these difficulties that you've already experienced, you should also be prepared for a few more: request limits in the browser, server-side performance concerns, and network infrastructure limitations.

Request Limits in the Browser

Playing with the application for any length of time will highlight another issue that is endemic to Comet and potentially more serious. In most modern web browsers, the number of concurrent HTTP connections to a given domain is limited to two. On an ordinary web site, this limit serves to queue requests in an orderly fashion without overwhelming the server, but when you're keeping requests open for long periods of time, it can have unexpected side effects.

Our Magnetic Poetry application will be making three types of request:

- Long polls to receive updates on the domain model, which may take up to a minute to return

- Comet requests to track the progress of the pottery baking process, which will take 30 seconds or more to complete

- Ordinary Ajax calls to notify the server of update, create, and delete operations that we have preformed

The long polls will be triggered automatically, and you can expect one of these requests to be running most of the time. If the user also orders a set of baked goods, she will be using up both her allotted HTTP connections for the next 30 seconds or so. Any create, update, or delete actions that you try to accomplish during this time will be suspended on the browser until an HTTP connection is free, making the application feel extremely sluggish and unresponsive. In Figure 3-3, we've captured this blocked Ajax request in the Firebug HTTP console. The first two open requests are a long poll and a Comet request, but the third is an ordinary Ajax request that is being blocked.

Figure 3-3. If more than one Comet request is being held open against a particular server, ordinary Ajax requests to that server will be blocked until one of the Comet requests closes.

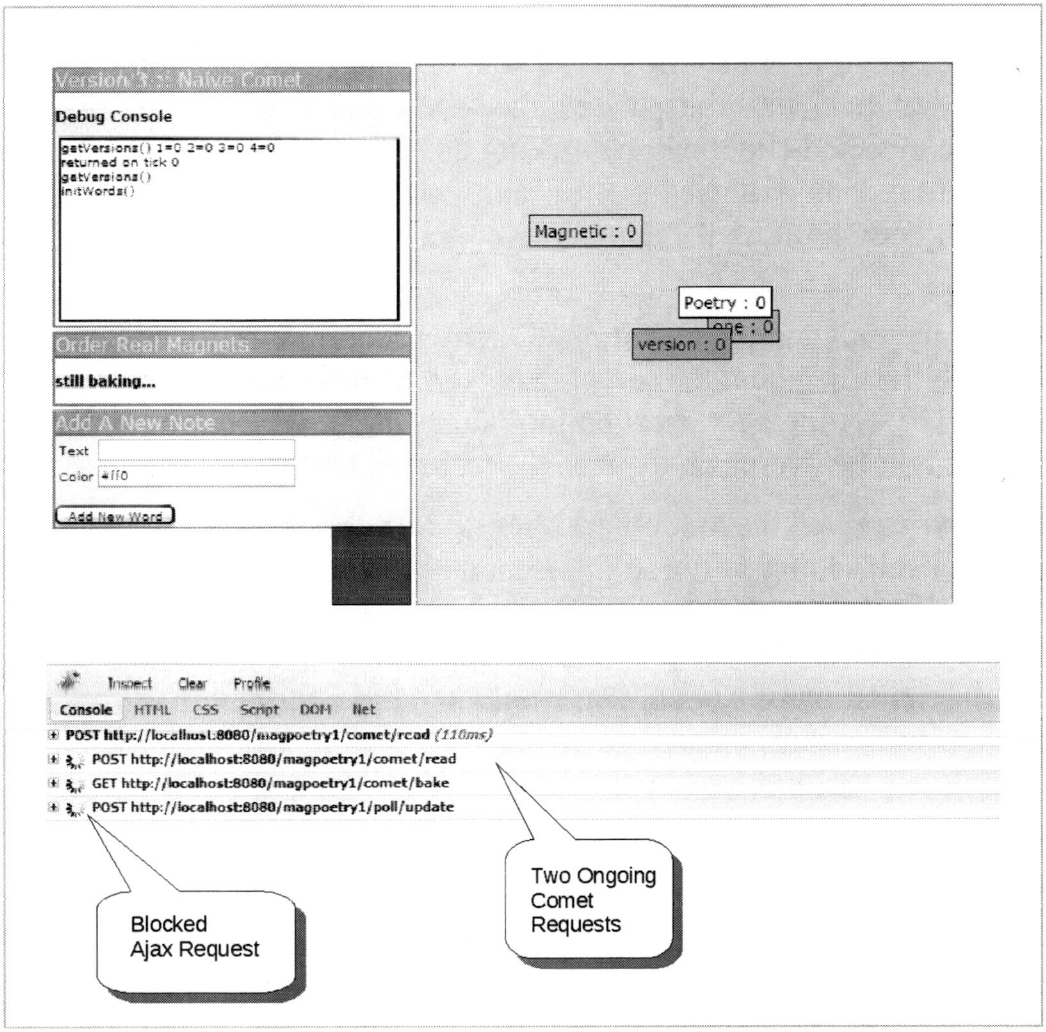

When using Comet, then, being careful about when you open Comet connections is imperative, and ideally, you should publish all Comet updates through a single common channel. You'll look at how to achieve this when we discuss DWR's implementation of Comet in Chapters 4 and 5 and the Bayeux protocol in Chapters 6 and 7.

Server-Side Performance Concerns

For both Comet and long polling, you kept your requests alive by suspending the thread in which the servlet was running. This will minimize the CPU load, but even while suspended, the servlet is still using memory. Further, each connected client will be making use of a servlet instance nearly all the time. You will need to provision your pool of servlets accordingly, thereby limiting the number of concurrent users that you can support.

Also note that the naive implementation of Comet required localized polling on both the client and the server. You can achieve a high level of responsiveness by setting very short polling intervals, if we gloss over the fact that you might be overusing expensive resources within the loop.

On the client, you polled the XHR object after it had achieved the interactive ready state. In itself, doing so doesn't present a problem. However, on the server, you polled the database frequently enough to give your DBA cause for concern about scalability. If you were to implement an efficient, scalable implementation of Comet, you would need to consider an event-driven mechanism, such as a message queue, for passing information on updates in a timely fashion.

Network Infrastructure

As if the preceding points weren't inconveniences enough, even the network infrastructure may misunderstand us when we're using Comet! Specifically, some proxy servers optimize performance by chunking responses (i.e., holding on to the data returned from the server until a sufficient volume has accumulated and then sending everything to the browser at once). If you're trying to drip-feed data along a Comet connection, chunking proxies can prove to be a great inconvenience.

Some of the more sophisticated Comet toolkits will attempt to diagnose the presence of proxies that behave in this way by sending test packets. If they find any, they fall back to a long-polling mechanism, but that functionality is quite out of the league of the naive Comet implementations introduced in this chapter.

To implement Comet properly, a comprehensive rethink about the architecture of our server, as well as the client, is required. An event-driven mechanism for communicating updates begins to look like a necessity, and ideally, you would like a more efficient means of suspending servlet instances and reducing their footprint while they are asleep. You're looking at changes not only to the application architecture but to the design of the web server itself.

Fortunately, work on these issues is underway, and the web server technologies required to implement scalable Comet are maturing rapidly. We'll turn to these issues in the remainder of this book, looking at the DWR toolkit in Chapters 4 and 5, and the Jetty server's Cometd implementation in Chapters 6 and 7.

Summary

In this chapter, you implemented a working Comet-based system from scratch. It was a heroic effort, but you encountered a number of interesting issues along the way that leave doubts about the robustness of such a solution. The effort that you've undertaken has been worthwhile, though, in bringing these issues to light. In the remainder of this book, you'll use this knowledge to understand how mature Comet implementations can achieve robustness and scalability.

Chapter 4: Comet the Easy Way

In the first chapter of this book, you were introduced to the basic concepts behind Comet and subsequently learned about the individual building blocks that fit together to form a working Comet stack. You saw in Chapter 2 how to open long-lived requests using XmlHTTPRequest or an iframe. Chapter 3 demonstrated how to keep requests open on the server and push out data as it arrives.

However, you also learned about some of Comet's complexities, such as the limit of two concurrent requests imposed by certain browsers, and some of the server-side scalability obstacles that long-lived requests present.

If you were feeling adventurous, you could now develop your own Comet application from scratch. Inevitably though, you'd spend at least as much time developing and debugging your Comet stack as you would on your application logic. Comet is a fairly outrageous hack, exploiting browser behavior and the HTTP protocol in ways that were never intended at their inception. As a result, pioneering Comet developers exploring this unfamiliar territory can expect to battle against browser quirks and oddities, misbehaving HTTP implementations, and a host of corner cases and unforeseen consequences.

In this chapter, we'll show you that there is an easier way using tools like Direct Web Remoting (DWR) that deal with many of the headaches of Comet development.

The Emergence of Comet Tools

Only a few years ago, Ajax was in a similar situation to that of Comet today—Ajax was a roll-your-own solution, and you had to worry about details like browser-dependent implementations of the XmlHTTPRequest object, how to construct requests, and how to parse responses. Fortunately, smart people very quickly built easy-to-use JavaScript libraries that abstracted away all of these worries, and today, very few developers would consider writing an Ajax application without relying on Dojo, Prototype, jQuery, and friends to take care of the heavy lifting.

With Comet, we can thankfully turn to these smart people again. Several libraries take care of the intricacies of parts of the Comet stack. On the client side, Dojo and jQuery offer Comet features, while the Meteor (`http://meteorserver.org/`) and Liberator (`http://freeliberator.com/`) servers are dedicated primarily to serving Comet requests. The Cometd project is also hard at work creating interoperable server-side and client-side Comet libraries based on the Bayeux protocol. You can learn about Bayeux in Chapter 6.

Arguably the most comprehensive and easy-to-use Comet implementation currently available is Getahead's DWR framework for the Java platform (`http://directwebremoting.org/`). DWR integrates Comet transparently into existing Java logic, allowing you to concentrate on simply writing your application functionality. It's a great choice when you need to have Comet closely integrated with your application logic—a setup that DWR's author Joe Walker calls onboard Comet.

We're going to use DWR to demonstrate how simply you can develop a Comet application when you don't have to worry about all of the complexity under the hood.

Direct Web Remoting

Before we begin, though, let's take a quick look into the history of DWR. DWR first emerged in early 2005 as a web remoting tool built on Ajax. In Java, the standard way of exposing behavior to the web is to write servlets, basically the Java equivalent of CGI scripts. Servlets parse HTTP request parameters, perform operations on server-side objects as required, and return an HTTP response representing the results of these operations, usually in the form of an HTML document.

Conceptually, DWR does away with the servlet layer and provides access directly from JavaScript calls in the web browser to methods on server-side Java objects. Therefore, developers using DWR can simply place all of their logic in server-side classes, rather than in script-like servlet code. They then configure DWR to expose the methods of these classes and automatically generate JavaScript representations of them to include in the application's web pages.

DWR in Action

To demonstrate the use of DWR, let's create a Java class called `DwrMagPoetryController`. This cut-down version of the Magnetic Poetry example application you encountered earlier in this book simply allows `Word` objects to be stored and retrieved. Here's the source code for the `DwrMagPoetryController` class:

```java
public class DwrMagPoetryController {

  public void addWord(Word word) {
    word.save();
  }

  public Collection<Word> findAllWords() {
    return Word.findAll();
  }
}
```

As you can see, there isn't much to it. The `Word` class incorporates methods that deal with the persistence concerns here. It's sufficient to know that we can either add a new `Word` object or retrieve all existing `Word` objects from the datastore.

Now, to expose these methods to calls from the browser, we need to configure DWR via the `dwr.xml` file. Here is the `dwr.xml` configuration for this example:

```
<dwr>
  <allow>
    <create creator="new" scope="application"
     javascript="DwrMagPoetry">
      <param name="class"
       value="comet.magpoetry.DwrMagPoetryController"/>
      <include method="addWord"/>
      <include method="findAllWords"/>
    </create>

    <convert converter="bean"
     match="comet.magpoetry.word.Word"/>
  </allow>
</dwr>
```

Inside the top-level `dwr` element is an `allow` element that tells DWR explicitly what its remoting mechanism should permit access to. Anything not included in the `allow` element is protected, meaning that you don't need to worry about accidentally exposing unintended functionality to hackers.

Two elements are nested inside `allow`: `create` and `convert`. The `create` element is how we tell DWR to expose a class for remoting, and it has three attributes: `creator`, `scope`, and `javascript`. The first attribute, `creator`, tells DWR how to instantiate the class in question; possible options include calls to factory classes or integration with Spring. Here, we simply want DWR to call `DwrMagPoetryController`'s constructor, so we specify `new`. We also only need a single instance of the class, which will live for the lifetime of the web application, so we set the `scope` attribute to `application`. Other possibilities here are to bind the created instance to a client's `HttpSession` or to create a new instance for each individual request. The final attribute, `javascript`, defines the name of the generated JavaScript object that web client code will interface with.

Enclosed within the `create` element is a parameter to tell DWR the fully qualified name of the class we're talking about and `include` elements to explicitly define which methods should be exposed. The `include` elements form a white list, meaning that any other methods on the class should not be remoted.

Now, if you look back to the signatures of the methods we are exposing, you'll see that one takes a `Word` instance as a parameter, and the other returns a `Collection` of `Word` instances. When it comes to passing objects back and forth between JavaScript code and Java code, DWR is pretty smart. Any of the basic Java types, like the primitives and `String`, are converted automatically, and `Collection` types are converted into JavaScript arrays. We do need to explain to DWR how to convert a custom type like `Word`, however.

Since `Word` follows the standard JavaBean semantics, all we have to do is specify that DWR should use its built-in introspection-based bean converter to bind values to and from web calls. In more complex cases, where bean introspection isn't sufficient to serialize the data from your objects, you can implement a custom `Convertor` yourself.

That's the DWR configuration dealt with. The only remaining task is to deploy the servlet component of DWR.

DWRServlet

DWRServlet is the intermediary between DWR's JavaScript code and your Java objects.

Here's the pertinent snippet from our web.xml configuration to set up DWR:

```
<servlet>
  <servlet-name>dwr-invoker</servlet-name>
  <servlet-class>
    org.directwebremoting.servlet.DwrServlet
  </servlet-class>
  <init-param>
    <param-name>debug</param-name>
    <param-value>true</param-value>
  </init-param>
</servlet>
<servlet-mapping>
  <servlet-name>dwr-invoker</servlet-name>
  <url-pattern>/dwr/*</url-pattern>
</servlet-mapping>
```

As well as mapping the DwrServlet to the /dwr/ URL, we've also enabled DWR's debug mode, which provides a very useful snapshot of the classes and methods that DWR is remoting and is invaluable during development. You just need to navigate to <your-web-app>/dwr/, where you will be presented with a list of remoted classes, as defined in dwr.xml. Clicking a class name takes you to a test page that looks like the one shown in Figure 4-1.

Figure 4-1. DWR's test page for DwrMagPoetry

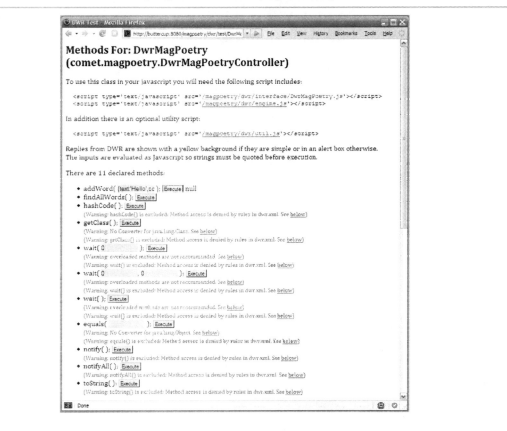

The first thing to note on the test page is the list of methods on the remoted class that specify whether access to each is permitted or denied. As expected, only addWord() and findAllWords() can be invoked. The test page allows you to make calls to these methods and see their return values too.

Where a method takes arguments, input boxes are provided to pass in JavaScript literals, which may be strings or numbers in simple cases. Since addWord expects a Word object, we can pass in a JavaScript object literal defining the properties of a Word, for instance, {text: 'Hello', color: '#ff0'}.

Clicking the Execute button invokes the method remotely. Since the addWord() method is void, DWR displays the return value null next to the method name once the call completes.

We can also call findAllWords() to ensure that the Word was correctly added to the datastore. Since this method returns a Collection of Word objects, DWR won't display its return value inline, and instead uses an alert dialogue, which is shown in Figure 4-2.

Figure 4-2. JSON output from findAllWords

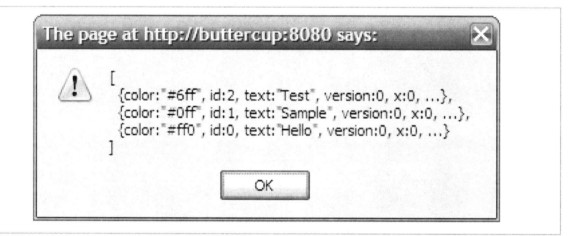

The debug screen also provides the scripts tags you need to include in your web pages to make calls on the remoted class:

```
<script type='text/javascript'
 src='/magpoetry/dwr/interface/DwrMagPoetry.js'>
</script>
<script type='text/javascript'
 src='/magpoetry/dwr/engine.js'>
</script>
```

DWR's engine.js contains the core client-side DWR functionality. The other JavaScript include, DwrMagPoetry.js, is automatically generated by

`DWRServlet`. It contains remote proxy objects representing each of the classes remoted by DWR.

When client-side code makes a function call on one of these JavaScript proxies, DWR's client-side engine is transparently invoked to make an HTTP call, via Ajax, to `DWRServlet`, which calls the corresponding Java object's method and returns its response wrapped in a JSON packet. Back in the browser, DWR unpacks the JSON response and passes the method's return value to a callback function. To the client, all of this looks like a simple asynchronous function call.

Here's an example that invokes the remoted `getAllWords()` function on our `DwrMagPoetry` instance from JavaScript:

```
DwrMagPoetry.getAllWords(function(words) {
  for (var word in words) {
    alert(word.text);
  }
});
```

DWR adds an optional callback parameter to the end of each remoted method's parameter list. This allows you to specify a function that the Java method's returned value will be passed to. In this case, the method returns a `Collection` of `Word` instances, which DWR converts into a JavaScript array of untyped JSON objects.

DWR also provides a simple call-batching mechanism to allow multiple Ajax calls to be executed in a single request, avoiding the two-connections-per-domain limitation.

```
DWREngine.beginBatch();
DwrMagPoetry.addWord({text:'Yellow',color:'#ff0'});
DwrMagPoetry.addWord({text:'Red',color:'#f00'});
DwrMagPoetry.addWord({text:'Green',color:'#0f0'});
DWREngine.endBatch();
```

None of these calls will be sent to the server until `endBatch()` is called. If the three batched remote calls included callbacks to handle return values, they would be invoked as normal, in order—DWR deals with multiplexing the batched responses transparently.

DWR and Comet

Version 2.0 of DWR introduces the concept of Reverse Ajax, in other words, the ability to invoke client-side behavior from the server side. Reverse Ajax is conceptually broader in scope than Comet, since its implementation in DWR allows the simulation of server push behavior with regular polling, request piggybacking, or Comet-style long polls. Indeed, one of the many benefits of using DWR over a nuts-and-bolts approach to Comet is that the chosen server push mechanism can be switched with a simple configuration change. Should you decide, for instance, that a 30-second interval between updates to your dynamic web page is perfectly acceptable, you can easily switch over to DWR's polling mechanism and reduce your server's traffic burden. The decision is just as easily reversed, without impacting your application design or architecture.

Magnetic Poetry Meets DWR on the Client Side

Let's now implement the Magnetic Poetry application from Chapter 2 using Reverse Ajax. Following on from our `DwrMagPoetryController` example, we will reuse the existing functionality of the `Word` class, allowing words to be saved and retrieved from storage. However, we will also add the ability to update or delete existing words. A new controller class called `ReverseAjaxController` will encapsulate all of our business logic.

`ReverseAjaxController` keeps the `findAllWords()` method from `DwrMagPoetryController`. Client web pages will call this method when they first load up to get the current state of the word datastore:

```
public Collection<Word> findAllWords() {
    return Word.findAll();
}
```

Users can then manipulate the virtual refrigerator door by adding new words, changing the properties of words already present, or deleting words. Here is a snippet of our Magnetic Poetry JavaScript code that illustrates calls on `ReverseAjaxController`'s methods:

```
function initWords(){
    ReverseAjaxController.findAllWords(function(words) {
        for (var i=0; i<words.length; i++) {
            new Word(words[i]);
        }
    }
    );
}

function addWord(){
    var text=$F('word_text');
    var color=$F('word_color');
    var x=Math.floor(Math.random()*350);
    var y=Math.floor(Math.random()*420);

    ReverseAjaxController.addWord(
        { text:text, color:color, x:x, y:y }
    );
}
```

The `initWords()` function is called on load, populating the client's view with all of the existing words in the Magnetic Poetry datastore. When the user adds a new word, we invoke DWR to make an Ajax call to `ReverseAjaxController`'s `addWord()` method. Deletion and modification of existing words are handled similarly.

Magnetic Poetry and DWR on the Server Side

On the server side, `ReverseAjaxController` responds to these events from the client with the methods `addWord()`, `deleteWord()`, and `updateWord()`. These methods persist the client's changes and notify all connected Magnetic Poetry clients of what happened. It's this notification step that relies on DWR's Reverse Ajax technology.

Here's `ReverseAjaxController` in full:

```
public class ReverseAjaxController {
  public Collection<Word> findAllWords() {
    return Word.findAll();
  }

  public void addWord(Word word) {
    word.save();
    notifyAllClients("wordAdded",word);
  }

  public void deleteWord(Word word) {
    word.delete();
    notifyAllClients("wordDeleted",word);
  }
  public void updateWord(Word word) {
    word.save();
    notifyAllClients("wordUpdated",word);
  }

  private void notifyAllClients(String eventType,
                                Word word) {
    getScriptProxy().addFunctionCall(eventType, word);
  }


  private ScriptProxy getScriptProxy() {
    WebContext ctx = WebContextFactory.get();
```

```
Collection sessions =
  ctx.getScriptSessionsByPage(ctx.getCurrentPage());

return new ScriptProxy(sessions);
    }
  }
```

The Reverse Ajax magic is all in the two private methods:
notifyAllClients() and getScriptProxy(). Each time a change
occurs that needs to be communicated to all connected clients, we call
notifyAllClients() with a String representing the change event and
the Word affected by the change.

In notifyAllClients(), the first action is to obtain a ScriptProxy, a
DWR object that allows JavaScript to be pushed to multiple clients. The
getScriptProxy() method uses DWR's WebContext to obtain a
ScriptSession for each browser currently viewing the Magnetic Poetry
web page. ScriptSession provides the underlying functionality for
passing scripts to a single client, but wrapping a collection of
ScriptSessions in a ScriptProxy provides convenience methods for
sending script to them all at once.

Two approaches can be used with ScriptProxy to execute JavaScript on
clients. ScriptProxy can be provided with the raw JavaScript in a
ScriptBuffer, which is essentially a StringBuffer with some DWR
niceties to convert Java data types into JSON literals. Alternatively, a
sequence of client-side JavaScript functions to be invoked can be specified
via calls to ScriptProxy's addFunctionCall() method.

Our notifyAllClients() uses the function-call approach. Our client-side
JavaScript code contains functions whose names correspond to the types of
word event that can occur: wordAdded(), wordDeleted(), and
wordUpdated(). Using ScriptProxy, a function call is generated
corresponding to the eventType parameter, and the affected Word object is
passed as an argument to that JavaScript function.

Here are our JavaScript implementations of these functions, each updating the user interface in response to the server's notification:

```
function wordAdded(wordProps) {
  new Word(wordProps);
}

function wordDeleted(wordProps) {
  var deleteMe = Words.getWordById(wordProps.id);
  deleteMe.deleteUI();
}

function wordUpdated(wordProps) {
  var updateMe = Words.getWordById(wordProps.id)
  updateMe.updateUI(wordProps.x,wordProps.y,
                              wordProps.version);
}
```

In each case, wordProps is a JSON representation of a server-side Java Word object that is automatically marshaled by DWR. This JSON representation is used to create or modify a corresponding JavaScript Word object.

Routing Magnetic Poetry Events

There's a design pattern here that is worth noting: while the user can manipulate controls on the page to create or modify words, his input does not directly modify the view. Instead, all that happens is that the ReverseAjaxController is notified of the user's intentions. Once the server-side model has been updated, the change event is pushed out to all clients, including the client that instigated the change. The user interface itself is only modified in response to calls on wordAdded(), wordDeleted(), and wordUpdated(). This series of interactions is illustrated in Figure 4-3.

Figure 4-3. Routing of events in the Reverse Ajax Magnetic Poetry application

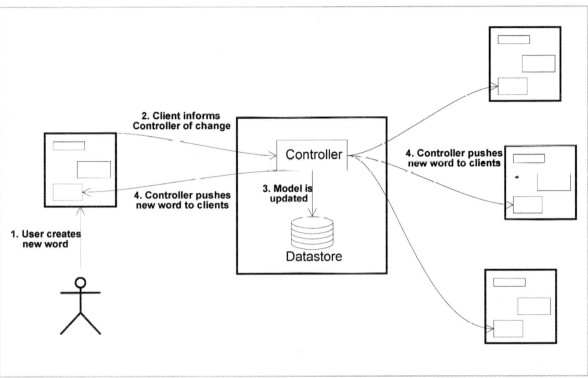

The advantage of the approach illustrated in Figure 4-3 is that it allows all clients to be treated uniformly, with no special cases for the client that instigated the changes. There's no special logic on either the client or server to differentiate the client making a change from clients that should be informed of the change. This technique also guarantees that all clients will be kept in sync, allowing conflicts between concurrent changes to be resolved on the server.

There's one small but vital detail of Reverse Ajax that we haven't discussed yet. Earlier, we showed how WebContext's getScriptSessionsByPage() method allows us to push JavaScript code out to all clients currently connected to the Magnetic Poetry page. But how does DWR know who these clients are? The answer is that all Reverse Ajax clients need to make a single DWR call when the page first loads:

```
dwr.engine.setActiveReverseAjax(true);
```

This call registers the client with DWR for push notifications. Under the hood, making this call initiates the long-lived requests that Comet relies on.

Wrapping Up This Implementation

To wrap up, let's take a look at our server-side configuration files for the Reverse Ajax example. First, here's dwr.xml:

```xml
<dwr>
  <allow>
    <create creator="new" scope="application"
     javascript="ReverseAjaxController" >
      <param name="class"
       value="comet.magpoetry.ReverseAjaxController"/>
      <include method="findAllWords"/>
      <include method="addWord"/>
      <include method="updateWord"/>
      <include method="deleteWord"/>
    </create>

    <convert converter="bean"
     match="comet.magpoetry.word.Word"/>
  </allow>
</dwr>
```

There is nothing out of the ordinary here; we just need to ensure that all of the server-side functions we require are exposed using the allow element. The convert element again informs DWR that Word should be serialized to JSON using standard JavaBean semantics.

Finally, one special change needs to be made in web.xml:

```
<servlet>
  <servlet-name>dwr-invoker</servlet-name>
  <servlet-class>
    org.directwebremoting.servlet.DwrServlet
  </servlet-class>
  <init-param>
    <param-name>activeReverseAjaxEnabled</param-name>
    <param-value>true</param-value>
  </init-param>
</servlet>
```

The `activeReverseAjaxEnabled` parameter determines what type of Reverse Ajax DWR will use. When the parameter is `false`, DWR will rely on piggybacking and will only publish server-side changes to clients when those clients themselves make an Ajax call to the server. In the Magnetic Poetry case, piggybacked events would mean that a user would only see other users' changes when she herself made a change.

That approach might be suitable for certain types of web applications, where prompt delivery of updates to clients isn't a priority. In our case, however, we need to enable active Reverse Ajax. In this mode, DWR will implement Reverse Ajax using Comet.

Summary

Comet is still an immature technology, based on unorthodox usage of the HTTP protocol that runs counter to many of the inherent assumptions in the conventional web stack. As a result, few of the web tools and libraries available are designed around implementing long-poll Comet applications, and developing your own stack is hard. However, Comet-centric tools are beginning to appear. In the Java world, DWR provides a simple and easy-to-use approach to general Ajax application development, providing good integration with existing Java technologies and automatically generating intuitive JavaScript code to call on the client side. Reverse Ajax takes this further, and makes Comet-based applications possible with only a few lines of configuration.

Chapter 5: Scaling Comet in Java

You've now seen how DWR integrates with Java applications to implement server push using Comet. But we haven't yet addressed scaling. In this chapter, we'll begin by examining why traditional web servers scale poorly to the demands of a Comet application. We'll then look at the Jetty server, which offers an alternative approach to serving Comet requests, and demonstrate how to write scalable Comet applications using this proprietary approach.

Thread Management for the Web

As you saw earlier in this book, traditional servers allocate a thread to each incoming HTTP request. The idea is that the thread should perform any necessary work to service the request and send a response as quickly as possible, after which it is allocated to another inbound request. This design works well when serving a large volume of short-lived requests—when quickly rendering simple dynamic web pages, for instance—and is commonly used with PHP, Ruby on Rails, and ASP, among many others.

Comet's traffic pattern is completely at odds with this approach, however. Long polls, by nature, are held open for a considerable length of time, and each Comet client will spend most of its time with a long-poll request in progress. This means that a Comet server needs to deal with as many concurrent requests as it has clients, and since every thread consumes considerable resources, the thread-per-request model is generally unable to scale to large numbers of clients. Consider also that a long-polling Comet request spends most of its life cycle in an idle state, merely waiting for an event to occur. No real work is being performed for that request, so tying up a thread only to do nothing with it is clearly inefficient.

Normally, Java servers use the thread-per-connection model. That is, each incoming HTTP connection is bound to a Java thread, and that thread is used to perform all work related to that connection. Once the connection is closed, the thread can be returned to a pool for reuse. Recently, servers have taken advantage of Java's asynchronous I/O APIs in order to move to event-driven connection handling. This allows a single thread to maintain many open connections, queuing their requests until they can be handled by servlet code (remember that in HTTP 1.1, several requests can be sent consecutively over a single connection).

However, the Java servlet model itself is inherently a thread-per-request design. When an HTTP request arrives at the servlet container, a thread is assigned to that request and is used to execute a servlet's instructions. Servlets lack any mechanism to pause, pending a server-side event, other than halting their thread of execution using the Java language's built-in `wait/notify` lock semantics.

Let's take a look at using `wait/notify` to suspend a request until a server-side event occurs. This is at the heart of any Comet-like long-polling call.

wait/notify

Returning to the Magnetic Pottery text-to-ceramics service you saw earlier, we'll start with a servlet that pulls a `String` parameter, `word`, from the `HttpServletRequest` and creates a `BakeryOrder` object from it. It then sends the order to the bakery and waits until the ceramic word is "baked."

```
public class MagneticPotteryServlet
                    extends HttpServlet {
  public void doGet(HttpServletRequest req,
                 HttpServletResponse res)
              throws ServletException, IOException {

    String wordToBake = req.getParameter("word");
```

```
    res.setContentType("text/plain");
    res.getWriter().println(
            new Date()+": Word to bake: "+wordToBake);
    res.flushBuffer();

    BakeryOrder order =
        new WaitNotifyBakeryOrder(wordToBake);
    Word baked = order.sendToBakery();

    res.getWriter().println(new Date()+": Done!");
  }
}
```

As you can see, nothing special is going on here: a synchronous call, `order.sendToBakery()`, is surrounded by some timestamps to show how long the process takes. Note that we flush the response buffer before making the `sendToBakery()` call, so that the first timestamp is output immediately.

`Bakery` itself runs in a constant loop, baking a fresh batch of words every 10 seconds. To have `Bakery` bake a `Word` for you, you call its `placeOrder()` method, passing in a `BakeryOrder`. When the `Word` that you ordered is baked, `Bakery` invokes `orderComplete()` on the `BakeryOrder`. Here are the interesting bits of `Bakery`'s implementation:

```
public class Bakery implements Runnable {

    private Set<BakeryOrder> nextBatch =
                        new HashSet<BakeryOrder>();

    void placeOrder(BakeryOrder order) {

      synchronized (nextBatch) {
        nextBatch.add(order);
      }
    }
}
```

```java
public void run() {
  while (true) {

    Set<BakeryOrder> currentBatch;
    synchronized(nextBatch) {
      currentBatch = nextBatch;
      nextBatch = new HashSet<BakeryOrder>();
    }
    try {
      // Simulate baking time
      Thread.sleep(10000);
    } catch (InterruptedException e) {}

    for (BakeryOrder order : currentBatch) {
      Word freshBakedWord =
              new Word(order.getTextToBake());
      order.orderComplete(freshBakedWord);
    }
  }
}
```

Again, this snippet is fairly straightforward. The Order objects passed to the placeOrder() method are accumulated in the nextBatch variable until the current batch is baked. After that, nextBatch becomes currentBatch; currentBatch is sent to bake for 10 seconds; and finally Order objects are notified that their fresh-baked words are ready. We just need to take care to synchronize on the nextBatch variable, because it is accessed by Bakery's own thread, as well as from client threads invoking placeOrder().

Finally, let's look at the implementation of WaitNotifyBakeryOrder. This class is responsible for adding itself to the Bakery's next batch of BakeryOrder objects and blocking until its orderComplete() callback is invoked by the Bakery.

Here's the code, with some minor details omitted:

```
class WaitNotifyBakeryOrder implements BakeryOrder {

  private Word bakedWord;
  private Object mutex = new Object();
  public Word sendToBakery() {

    synchronized (mutex) {
      Bakery.getInstance().placeOrder(this);

      while (bakedWord == null) {
        try {
          mutex.wait();
        } catch (InterruptedException e) {}
      }
    }

    return bakedWord;
  }

  public void orderComplete(Word bakedWord) {
    synchronized (mutex) {
      this.bakedWord = bakedWord;
      mutex.notify();
    }
  }
}
```

When sendToBakery() is called, WaitNotifyBakeryOrder passes itself
to the Bakery's placeOrder() method and waits on the mutex object until
bakedWord is set. Meanwhile, in the Bakery's execution thread, the order
will be processed and the orderComplete method called with the baked
Word object. This callback initializes the bakedWord member before using
mutex.notify() to signal the waiting thread to continue. Back in the
resumed sendToBakery() method, the baked Word is returned to the
caller, in our case MagneticPotteryServlet.

Here's the output from a call to `MagneticPotteryServlet`:

```
$ links
http://localhost:8080/magpoetry/pottery?word=WaitNotify

Sun Mar 02 22:02:49 GMT 2008: Word to bake: 'WaitNotify'
Sun Mar 02 22:03:05 GMT 2008: Done!
```

As you can see, in this particular case, it took 16 seconds for the request to be processed—6 seconds waiting for the `Bakery` to complete its previous batch and 10 seconds in the oven. This `wait/notify` approach works perfectly well for any given request being processed. The problem is one of scalability.

Difficulties in Using wait/notify with Comet

A servlet's thread is tied up for several seconds while the word is being baked, even though that thread is not doing any useful work. It's merely hanging around until it receives notification that the `Bakery` has completed its task, and it's not able to service other requests in the meantime. A large number of simultaneous requests to the `Bakery` class from Comet clients would therefore quickly exhaust the server's thread pool, resulting in long waits for threads to become available. You might conclude, therefore, that the thread-per-request Java servlet model is inherently unsuitable for large-scale Comet-type applications, because it doesn't scale well.

The root of the issue is that the Java servlet model was developed to serve a very different traffic profile, long before anyone had conceived of Comet-style asynchronous event delivery to the browser. Moreover, this thread-per-request model remains suitable for the vast majority of web applications, so there is little incentive to drastically alter it.

However, efforts have been made recently in the Java community to provide more Comet-friendly server architectures. Among these are Jetty 6, Grizzly (part of the GlassFish project), and Tomcat 6, each of which provides proprietary extensions to the regular servlet model to provide nonblocking, event-driven request processing. In the longer term, the Java Servlet specification itself will be enhanced with Comet-friendly features in version 3.0. You can read about the Servlet 3.0 proposals later in this chapter, but for now let's take a look at the Comet features in Jetty.

Jetty 6

Version 6 of WebTide's venerable Jetty server (http://www.mortbay.org/jetty-6/) introduced several innovations aimed at scaling long-lived requests. Many of these are under-the-hood implementation details, but the headline feature for any aspiring Comet developer is what WebTide calls continuations. Now, the term "continuation" is fairly loaded. Some people are familiar with continuations as language-level features (for instance, in Scheme and Ruby) that allow the current state of a computation to be encapsulated as a first-class data type. Meanwhile, in the Java world, Spring WebFlow uses the term to describe its mechanism for tracking conversational state in a web application. Jetty's use of the continuation is quite distinct from either of these: in simple terms, a Jetty continuation simply provides an alternative wait/notify mechanism that doesn't consume a server thread.

Using Jetty Continuations

However, employing continuations is a little more complex than using wait/notify, so let's take a look at how Jetty continuations are implemented. First of all, let's revisit the earlier MagneticPotteryServlet example—rewritten to use continuations. This example will work exactly like the earlier version except that the servlet's thread will be returned to the pool when the Bakery begins to process an order, and only when the order is complete will a thread again be consumed to continue servicing the request.

Here is the updated `MagneticPotteryServlet` code:

```
public class MagneticPotteryServlet
                    extends HttpServlet {

    public void doGet(HttpServletRequest req,
                    HttpServletResponse res)
                throws ServletException, IOException {

        String wordToBake = req.getParameter("word");

        res.setContentType("text/plain");
        res.getWriter().println(new Date() +
            ": Word to bake: '"+wordToBake+"'\n");
        res.flushBuffer();

        Continuation c =
            ContinuationSupport.getContinuation(req,null);

        BakeryOrder order =
                new ContinuationBakeryOrder(c,wordToBake);

        Word baked = order.sendToBakery();
        res.getWriter().println(new Date()+": Done!");
    }
}
```

The main difference from the original that you can see here is the extra step to obtain a `Continuation` instance from `HttpServletRequest`. You need this step because `Continuation` instances are intrinsically tied to the servlet request cycle, rather than being a general-purpose concurrency tool that can be conjured anywhere in your code. We've also implemented a new type of `BakeryOrder`, `ContinuationBakeryOrder`, which is initialized with the `Continuation` that we just obtained. Here's the implementation of `ContinuationBakeryOrder`, again with some details omitted:

```java
class ContinuationBakeryOrder implements BakeryOrder {

  Continuation continuation;

  public Word sendToBakery() {

    if (!continuation.isPending()) {
      Bakery.getInstance().placeOrder(this);
    }

    continuation.suspend(0);

    return (Word)continuation.getObject();
  }

  public void orderComplete(Word bakedWord) {
    continuation.setObject(bakedWord);
    continuation.resume();
  }
}
```

Let's examine the differences between this code and the earlier
WaitNotifyBakeryOrder. First of all, the calls to wait() and notify()
are replaced by calls to suspend() and resume() on the continuation
member variable. The argument supplied to the suspend() call is a
timeout parameter. Passing in zero means that the suspend() operation
will never time out and should wait to be explicitly resumed. The
synchronized blocks are gone too, as you don't need to obtain the
monitor of a Continuation as you would before invoking a Java object's
wait() or notify() method. Instead, a Continuation employs its own
alternative to Java's threading mechanisms, as you'll learn shortly.

Also, in the orderComplete() callback, note that a Continuation
instance has a handy way to store a context object, with setObject().
Using this context eliminates the need for a separate bakedWord property
on the ContinuationBakeryOrder, as the Word can be passed between

threads inside the `Continuation`—the `Word` is retrieved after the `suspend()` call using `getObject()`. Finally, and most significantly, the continuation-based approach requires a check of the `Continuation`'s `isPending()` method prior to the `sendToBakery()` call. Before we look into why that is, let's first consider the output from this reconfigured servlet, which provides some insight:

```
$ links
localhost:8080/magpoetry/pottery?word=Continuation

Sun Mar 02 22:06:28 GMT 2008: Word to bake: Continuation
Sun Mar 02 22:06:45 GMT 2008: Word to bake: Continuation
Sun Mar 02 22:06:45 GMT 2008: Done!
```

You'll no doubt spot that the first line of output is repeated, with a different timestamp, just before the "Done!" message is generated. This repetition is a big clue to how continuations are implemented.

Understanding the Continuation Mechanism

Like much of the Comet stack, continuations are actually something of a hack, bending the rules of existing technologies to provide the necessary functionality. Here's the trick behind a `Continuation`'s behavior: calling `suspend()` actually aborts processing of the servlet thread altogether, by throwing the Jetty-specific runtime exception `RetryRequest`. This exception propagates up into Jetty's internals, where the `Continuation` is extracted from the `RetryRequest` and put on ice in a queue with other suspended `Continuation` objects. Jetty is then able to use a single housekeeping thread to periodically run through all of the suspended `Continuation` objects in its queue, checking each to see whether each one's `resume()` method has been called from another thread.

When Jetty finds that a `Continuation` has been resumed, it replays the `Continuation`'s associated request: a thread is obtained from the pool and is used to invoke the servlet's doGet() (or doPost()) method exactly as it was when the request was initially received. This explains the double output from the servlet: this line of servlet code was executed twice.

Now, we obviously don't want the replayed request to do *exactly* what it did before, or we'll end up resubmitting our Word to the Bakery—this is where the Continuation's isPending() method comes in. It is used to distinguish requests that are being replayed from ones that are making their first visit to the servlet. The rule is that isPending() returns true if and only if suspend has already been called. In ContinuationBakeryOrder, we check for this condition and skip sending the order to the Bakery, returning the baked Word instead.

The key word here is "idempotence," meaning to have the same effect whether applied once or multiple times. An operation in Java is generally idempotent if multiple calls to it produce the same result each time, and the call doesn't have side effects. For instance, the call to request.getParameter("word") is idempotent here, since the result is exactly the same no matter how many times the operation is repeated. However, the status message output is not idempotent. It has the side effect of adding text to the servlet response stream, so performing it many times causes a different outcome than performing it only once. Strictly speaking, we should have made that status message conditional on the Continuation's isPending() state too. So, the general rule of thumb with continuations is that any code prior to your suspend() call must either be idempotent or conditional on isPending().

Look back to the output of the continuation-enabled MagneticPotteryServlet, and you'll see that it took 17 seconds to process. However, between the first timestamp at 22:06:28 and the second at 22:06:45, this request was suspended and not consuming a servlet thread. During this 17-second interval, a thread that would otherwise have been tied up idling in a wait() call was instead available to process other incoming requests or other continuations as they were resumed.

Using a Jetty Continuation means that a waiting request only consumes a slot in Jetty's pending continuations queue, rather than tying up an entire thread. This is great for Comet applications, as the number of requests waiting on events is no longer limited by the number of available threads.

Drawbacks of Continuations

Measurements of Jetty's Comet performance by WebTide developer Greg Wilkins reveal what a major difference continuations can make. In Wilkins's test, generating 10,600 concurrent requests without continuations caused Jetty to spawn 10,600 threads, with a consumption of 694MB of stack memory. Enabling continuations in the same scenario allowed Jetty to service the same number of requests with only 875 threads and 57MB of stack memory, while still servicing 5,000 requests per second. Clearly, this kind of scalability makes Java a viable solution for Comet after all.

However, there are a few drawbacks to using continuations in your web application. First of all, the continuation abstraction leaks slightly, meaning that your application code becomes polluted with continuation-related concerns. As you've seen, idempotence needs to be considered, and code made conditional on a Continuation's state where appropriate, which makes continuations-based code somewhat tricky to write.

There is also the issue of portability. The Continuations API is proprietary to Jetty, so you can't take continuations-dependent code and deploy to just any server. Technically, you can distribute the Jetty Continuations library with your web application, but in a non-Jetty environment, continuations fall back to providing a simple wrapper around wait/notify; it's Jetty's own servlet container that provides the true nonblocking continuation mechanism. Another approach is to use Java's Reflection API to detect whether continuations are available at runtime and dynamically switch between using a Continuation or wait/notify semantics. This makes your code truly portable, as the Continuations API is not required at runtime.

Jetty Continuations and DWR

While the extra programming overhead threatens to spoil the continuations party somewhat, a Comet solution makes continuations very easy to use: DWR. That's right; DWR's Reverse Ajax technology uses the reflection trick to transparently detect and use continuations for long polling when available, with no changes required to your application code. You don't need to worry about idempotence or portability; just write your Reverse Ajax application, and let DWR take care of the rest.

We now have all of the pieces in place to build a scalable Comet application using Reverse Ajax and Jetty continuations. All that's needed is to configure DWR and Jetty correctly, and the Reverse Ajax Magnetic Poetry example can scale to handle many simultaneous clients.

As you have already seen, only a single parameter needs to be set in web.xml for DWR to use Comet: activeReverseAjaxEnabled.

```
<servlet>
  <servlet-name>dwr-invoker</servlet-name>
  <servlet-class>
    org.directwebremoting.servlet.DwrServlet
  </servlet-class>
  <init-param>
    <param-name>activeReverseAjaxEnabled</param-name>
    <param-value>true</param-value>
  </init-param>
</servlet>
```

On the Jetty side, we just need to check that the server is configured to use nonblocking I/O, with the SelectChannelConnector. This is defined in Jetty's etc/jetty.xml configuration file:

```
<Call name="addConnector">
  <Arg>
    <New class=
      "org.mortbay.jetty.nio.SelectChannelConnector">
      <Set name="host">
        <SystemProperty name="jetty.host" />
      </Set>
      <Set name="port">
        <SystemProperty name="jetty.port"
         default="8080"/>
      </Set>
      <Set name="maxIdleTime">30000</Set>
      <Set name="Acceptors">2</Set>
      <Set name="statsOn">false</Set>
      <Set name="confidentialPort">8443</Set>
      <Set name="lowResourcesConnections">5000</Set>
      <Set name="lowResourcesMaxIdleTime">5000</Set>
    </New>
  </Arg>
</Call>
```

These settings are actually taken from the default setup on our build of Jetty, so no change was needed. The Magnetic Poetry application should now be able to scale to many hundreds of clients without breaking sweat.

Future Comet Support in Java

Earlier, we mentioned that other server vendors have also been looking into the scalability problems posed by Comet. In addition to WebTide's Comet work with continuations in Jetty, Sun's Grizzly project (https://grizzly.dev.java.net/) and Tomcat 6 (http://tomcat.apache.org/) both offer Comet support using their own proprietary APIs. For Java developers wishing to create scalable Comet applications, using a proprietary API is less than ideal, as Comet code written against Tomcat, Jetty, or Grizzly will not be portable to one of the other servers.

One of the goals of the Servlet 3.0 proposal, currently working its way through the Java Community Process as JSR 315, is to finally standardize asynchronous I/O and Comet support. Once the specification is finalized, nonblocking Comet support should become widespread among all Java server vendors, and most likely, Grizzly, Tomcat, and Jetty will all implement Servlet 3.0 too.

JSR 315 still has a long way to go, however. In the meantime, using DWR as an abstraction over the underlying Comet technology provides insulation from ongoing change. At the time of this writing, DWR 2 implements only Jetty 6's proprietary Continuations API for nonblocking Comet. However, DWR 3 will be available later in 2008 and will also provide support for both nonblocking Comet in Tomcat 6 and Grizzly. DWR will also work with Servlet 3.0 servers, once the specification is finished.

WebTide is preparing a major new release of Jetty (version 7). Currently available as an early prerelease, Jetty 7 offers an alternative to its tricky exception-based Continuations API. The Jetty 6–style API is still available in Jetty 7, however, so DWR will continue to be compatible with Jetty.

Summary

Comet traffic is inherently at odds with the conventional web paradigm where requests are short-lived and dealt with as quickly as possible by the server. Instead, Comet requests often need to be held open for a long time, albeit in an idle state. As a result, you've seen that conventional Java servlet engines do not scale efficiently to the traffic pattern peculiar to long-polling Comet applications.

However, efforts are underway to provide mechanisms to circumvent the blocking-thread-per-request model. You've seen Jetty 6's approach in continuations, which provide a highly scalable, if somewhat quirky, method of implementing event-driven web code.

Combining the strengths of DWR with Jetty 6 results in probably the best-integrated Comet implementation in Java, allowing us to concentrate on writing business logic while the details of long-polling schemes, data exchange protocols, and scalability are all dealt with almost transparently.

As Comet technology becomes more widespread, the Servlet 3.0 specification promises to unite server vendors under a common API. Until that time, the DWR project is working toward compatibility with the major Comet implementations in Jetty, Tomcat, and Grizzly.

Chapter 6: Introducing Bayeux

The technologies that we looked at in the previous chapter, Jetty continuations and DWR, simplify Comet enormously, and make it more robust than our hand-rolled efforts in Chapters 1 through 3. Yet these are proprietary stacks. If you want to use DWR's Reverse Ajax features, you need to adopt DWR as a central part of your architecture.

To some extent, using proprietary stacks is inevitable, and we certainly don't want to criticize projects that use them. However, there is a strong culture of open standards within the web development community. Standards promise freedom from vendor lock-in and real interoperability (and sometimes deliver on those promises!).

There is an emerging de facto standard for Comet. It is called Bayeux and has a formal specification document, the gruesome details of which can be found at `http://svn.xantus.org/shortbus/trunk/bayeux/bayeux.html`. The Bayeux specification itself is very generic, but there is also a reference implementation known as Cometd, for which working code is available in a variety of server-side languages. The Bayeux specification and some of the reference implementations of Cometd are provided by the people at Sitepen, who also gave us the Dojo JavaScript toolkit. We're going to look at Bayeux in this chapter (and rub shoulders with Dojo a bit along the way).

The first thing you need to know about this standard is what it covers and what it leaves out. What aspects of Comet does Bayeux standardize? We'll start by running through the specification itself and then move on to look at implementations.

HTTP Request Management

In Chapter 3, you encountered the limit of two concurrent HTTP connections to a server imposed by most web browsers. Because Comet request streaming and long-polling techniques keep requests open for a significant amount of time, ad hoc use of Comet requests can easily consume both these requests indefinitely, preventing images and other resources from loading and blocking ordinary Ajax calls (see Figure 3-3).

We suggested at the time that if you wished to support multiple Comet requests, you could channel them all through a single request. DWR's Reverse Ajax does this for you under the hood, but you didn't need to look at the implementation details.

Bayeux adopts exactly the same approach and provides a flexible, scalable API based around a publish-subscribe model. But there's only one HTTP request present, so what exactly do you subscribe to?

Data sent over Bayeux is always assigned a notional "channel." In reality, the channel is just a property assigned to each chunk of data (we'll look at the message format shortly), but you can think of the channels as discrete streams of data being carried within the single Comet request or response.

What does this look like in practice, then? Let's return to the Magnetic Poetry example, as presented in Figure 2-1, in which you wanted to receive Comet notifications for two purposes: getting updates on the progress of the ceramic bakery and being notified of changes that other users have made to the board.

In the overall design of the application, these two requirements are orthogonal. That is, you should be able to present a bakery component or a board component to the user independently of each other. Although they are required to share an HTTP transport, you can represent this orthogonality by assigning them to separate data channels. So, the bakery component will subscribe to a bakery channel, and see only bakery-related messages from the server, and the board component will subscribe to a board channel, and see only board-related messages.

On the server, you can send messages to either component simply by publishing them to a specific channel and be assured that only the appropriate component will receive them. On the client, the Bayeux implementation will serve as a shared dispatch mechanism for requests, and on the server, a similar shared dispatch mechanism will be needed. Behind these, you can produce a well-factored codebase on both client and server, as illustrated in Figure 6-1.

Figure 6-1. Bayeux's concept of channels allows multiple decoupled conversations on top of a single HTTP connection. The client-side Cometd object and server-side Bayeux implementation communicate over several notional channels all bundled within a single HTTP request-response pair.

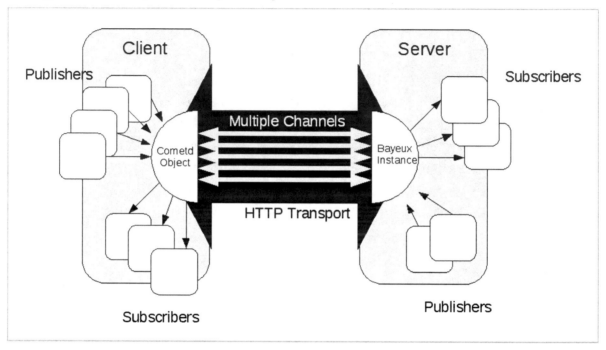

Naming Channels

Bayeux is very flexible and allows you free choice in naming channels, though the convention is to name channels in the style of Unix file paths. For example, we could call our bakery channel /magpoetry/bakery and the board updates channel /magpoetry/board.

The path-style convention allows us to organize channels hierarchically. Further, simple globbing-style wildcards are permitted. For example, a client could subscribe to the channel /magpoetry/*, in order to receive updates on /magpoetry/bakery, /magpoetry/board, and any other channels that started with that root. A single wildcard will only match one extra leg to the path. If we wanted to receive messages from /magpoetry/bakery/cake and magpoetry/bakery/danish/pastry, for example, we could do so using a double wildcard by subscribing to /magpoetry/**.

It's worth noting that channel names, like Unix paths and URLs, are case-sensitive. Messages to channel /magPoetry/fridge will not be received by a client subscribed only to /magpoetry/*.

Message Format

So we like the high-level abstraction of channels, but in reality, as we noted, all messages are flowing over a single transport and are assigned to channels purely by a property. What does a Bayeux message look like then? At this point, we're going to stick our heads under the hood of the Cometd engine to see what makes it tick. If you're curious about how Bayeux is designed, keep on reading. If you just want to get coding now, skip to the next section on Cometd implementations and come back here later.

The first thing to note about Bayeux is that it has standardized on JSON as the low-level serialization format for messages. JSON is a simple, flexible text-based markup that is well supported by JavaScript and its cousins ActionScript and ECMAScript and is currently very popular in the Ajax world.

JSON is sent in both directions: in the HTTP request and in the response. When publishing a message from a browser, the outgoing message is sent as a POST variable with name message. The JSON will typically detail the following fields:

- The message data, which may be an arbitrarily complex JSON data structure

- The channel that the message is being sent to, as a string

- A unique ID assigned to the client for the duration of a session

- A second unique ID for the message itself, usually a simple counter.

Let's look at a simple example. If we send some information about this book to the channel /apress/firstPress, we might see the following:

```
[
  {
    "data":{
      "title":"Comet & Reverse Ajax",
      "authors": [ "Dave", "Phil" ]
    },
    "channel":"/apress/firstPress",
    "clientId":"chcwmd0jx3nu",
    "id":"4"
  }
]
```

The top-level object is an array, containing a single object with the four properties mentioned previously. The data property is moderately complex, but the others are simple strings.

In response to publishing this message, we might receive a response of this type:

```
[
  {
    "id":"4",
    "successful":true,
    "channel":"/stuff/specific"
  },
  {
    "id":"4",
    "data":{
```

```
      "title":"Comet & Reverse Ajax",
      "authors": [ "Dave", "Phil" ]
    },
    "channel":"/apress/firstPress",
  }
]
```

Note that the response contains an array of two objects: a header and a body. The header contains details of the transaction, such as the unique message ID and whether the message succeeded in being published. The body, in this case, simply returns the data that was published to the channel, along with the ID and channel. These might look to be repeats of the data in the header, but that's only the case when we're receiving notification of a message that we published ourselves.

The same JSON format will be used when we connect to a Comet server in order to receive updates. If you look at the response received from such a request, you can see that the header information refers to the sender, and the body to the recipients. Here's a simple example.

```
[
  {
    "id":"18",
    "successful":true,
    "channel":"/meta/connect"
  },
  {
    "id":"15",
    "data":"hello world",
    "channel":"/apress/firstPress"
  }
]
```

The sender is the Comet process running on the server side, responding to the subscription via the channel /meta/connect (more on the metachannels in the next section), with the same message ID that you sent when you connected to the channel. Note that these message IDs will increment every time a new connection is made and are usually simple integers. Each instance of a Bayeux client is also assigned a unique client ID, which it maintains throughout its lifetime. Together, the message ID and client ID serve to uniquely identify a message.

In the body of the message, you receive the data that has been forwarded to you from another client, along with the message ID used by that client to publish the data, and the channel on which it published it. So, the header gives you information about which of your subscriptions the server is responding to, and the body gives information about the sender of the message.

Standard Channels

Within the flexible naming scheme provided by Bayeux, there is one reserved area. Any channel beginning with the word /meta is deemed to be used by the protocol itself, to perform connection handshaking, establishing subscriptions, and so on. We've already seen a response on the /meta/connect channel, being returned from a subscription to a channel.

In fact, whenever we open a Comet connection, we are sending a message to the /meta/connect channel. The POST body of a Comet request might look like this:

```
[
  {
    "channel":"/meta/connect",
    "connectionType":"long-polling",
    "clientId":"chcwmd0jx3nu",
    "id":"18"
  }
]
```

The properties `channel`, `clientId`, and `messageId` are familiar to us already. The fourth parameter, `connectionType`, is used to instruct the server on what type of Comet connection we are seeking to establish. In this case, we're requesting the long polling technique that we discussed in Chapter 3. The current specification mentions four connection types. Long polling and callback polling must be supported by all clients. Use of alternative transports such as iframes (see Chapter 3) and the binary Flash remoting protocol built into recent versions of Adobe's Flash and Flex products are cited as optional.

Transport Negotiation

In addition to the `/meta/connect` channel, the specification defines a `/meta/handshake` channel, through which a Comet client and server first establish communication, and negotiate the best kind of connection that they can support (this may depend on limitations in the client and server implementations themselves, factors related to their environment, and characteristics of the network such as the presence of proxy servers).

When connecting to a Cometd server, a client exchanges two messages over the `/meta/handshake` channel. First, it tells the server what capabilities it supports:

```
[
  {
    "version":"1.0",
    "minimumVersion":"0.9",
    "channel":"/meta/handshake",
    "id":"0",
    "ext":{
      "json-comment-filtered":true
    },
```

```
    "supportedConnectionTypes":[
        "long-polling",
        "callback-polling"
    ]
  }
]
```

The server replies by telling the client what its own version number is and what transports it supports. It also assigns it a unique client ID for the duration of the session and offers advice on how to connect. In the following example, the advice object is telling the client to connect for up to 4 minutes at a time (i.e., 240,000 milliseconds), without an interval between closing one connection and opening another:

```
[
  {
    "id":"0",
    "minimumVersion":"0.9",
    "supportedConnectionTypes":[
      "long-polling",
      "callback-polling"
    ],
    "successful":true,
    "channel":"/meta/handshake",
    "advice":{
        "reconnect":"retry",
        "interval":0,
        "timeout":240000
    },
    "clientId":"chcwmd0jx3nu",
    "version":"1.0"
  }
]
```

The client will then reply with a second message to /meta/handshake, in which it informs the server of its chosen connection method, usually by picking the best of the connection types offered by the server's previous response. It uses the `clientId` assigned by the server and will continue to do so in all future interactions:

```
[
    {
        "channel":"/meta/connect",
        "clientId":"chcwmd0jx3nu",
        "connectionType":"long-polling",
        "id":"1"
    }
]
```

If the server responds with a successful message, the connection between the client and server has been established, and the client can begin to subscribe to channels and publish to them. Here is the server's final response in the handshake:

```
[
    {
        "id":"1",
        "successful":true,
        "advice":{
            "reconnect":"retry",
            "interval":0,
            "timeout":240000
        },
        "channel":"/meta/connect"
    }
]
```

The server simply repeats its advice to the client at this stage, and the handshake is completed.

We've given you enough details about the specification. Now let's have a look at some real-world implementations.

Client-Side Implementations

Bayeux provides us with a complete protocol for passing data along Comet connections, but the protocol on its own is quite complex, and few of us would relish sitting down to write an implementation (or two, if we consider the client and server!) before being able to exchange any data. Fortunately, the Cometd project gives us off-the-shelf implementations that can transparently handle the handshaking, client IDs, and connection types, leaving us free to concentrate on the business data. In the remainder of this chapter, we'll look at two of the most popular Cometd implementations and see how we can use them to get some real work done with minimum effort.

Starting on the client side, we're going to look at the Cometd client that ships with the Dojo JavaScript framework. Dojo and Comet have a long shared history, both having sprung from the pen of Alex Russell and his colleagues at Sitepen. Dojo has something of a reputation as a large and complex client-side library. However, especially since version 0.9, Dojo has had an extremely modular structure, and the Cometd authors have been kind enough not to link their implementation too deeply into many other features of the toolkit. As a result, the Dojo Cometd client can be used successfully without a deep understanding of Dojo, and it plays well with other JavaScript libraries such as Prototype and jQuery.

You'll learn to need a little Dojo to get started, however, so let's get coding. First, you need to import the Dojo core libraries into your page, using a script tag, like so:

```
<script type="text/javascript"
  src="js/dojo/dojo/dojo.js.uncompressed.js">
</script>
```

We've referenced a copy of `dojo.js` on your local server in order to keep the downloadable code for this book complete. However, the full Dojo library is available on AOL's content delivery network, so you may choose to reference that and Comet-enable your application without having to install any Dojo on your server at all. The full URL to Dojo version 1.0 is

```
http://o.aolcdn.com/dojo/1.0.0/dojo/dojo.xd.js
```

This loads the basic Dojo capabilities into your browser but no Cometd client. To get hold of that code, you need a second script tag, but not one pointing to another external URL. Rather, you should call Dojo's `require()` method, which will load the extra code using Ajax, pulling in any dependencies needed (in this case, there are none), and evaluate it for you.

Once you have loaded Dojo's Comet implementation in this way, we can initialize it in one line of code, at which point it will perform the handshake for us:

```
<script type="text/javascript">
   dojo.require("dojox.cometd");
   dojox.cometd.init("cometd");
   //do some more comet
</script>
```

Dojo's codebase is well organized into a number of namespaces. The namespace `dojo` covers core capabilities, and `dojox` the nonstandard extensions, in much the same way that the Sun JRE's `java.*` and `javax.*` packaging conventions work. The Cometd classes are found under the namespace `dojox.comet`.

The argument that you pass to the `init()` method of the `dojox.cometd` object is a URL at which the Cometd server can be found. In this case, that's a very simple relative URL.

Using the `dojox.comet` object, you can now subscribe to and unsubscribe from channels, and publish messages. The first thing you'll want to do with your Comet capabilities is to subscribe to a channel. The subscription operation is essentially asynchronous and will therefore require you to provide callback code to handle messages delivered on the channel once you have subscribed. In many JavaScript libraries, callbacks are handled by passing a `Function` object as an argument, but the Dojo comet classes take a slightly different approach. The easiest way to see how this works is by example, so let's get started.

The `dojox.comet` object provides a `subscribe()` method that takes four arguments. The first is the name of the channel that you want to subscribe to, which is what we expect. The second and third handle the callback: they are the object that will handle the callback and the name of the method of the object that should be called, respectively. The fourth argument is a configuration object allowing you to set properties of the message. This can be left as null in most ordinary cases.

Let's look at an example subscription:

```
dojox.cometd.subscribe(
  '/apress/firstPress',
  myObject,
  'handleMessage'
)
```

To complete the code, you need to supply an object with an appropriately named method, so we could write one like this:

```
var myObject={
  handleMessage:function(msg){
    alert(msg.channel+" says "+dojo.toJson(msg.data));
  }
}
```

Let's stop to examine the argument passed into the callback function. You can see from the preceding example that it has `data` and `channel` properties. Looking back to our earlier discussion of Bayeux message types, you can see that this is in fact the body of the Bayeux message (that is, the second element in the array). In most cases, though, the interesting property will be the data, which, as we saw earlier, can be as simple or as complex as you like it to be.

Note that the callback function provided here will be called when another client publishes a message to the channel, not in response to the subscription being made over the /meta/connect channel. We did discuss what that response looked like in terms of the Bayeux protocol, but the details of it are hidden from you when you use the dojox.comet classes.

Now you can publish messages to the channel. Let's do that next. Unsurprisingly, you can find a method on dojox.comet called publish(). It takes two arguments: the channel to publish over and the data to send. As with subscribe(), a third argument can be provided if you want to configure the transmission, but stick with the defaults for now.

The second argument is a JavaScript object, as simple or as complex as you want it to be. You should, however, note that the object should contain only data, not behavior, as it's going to be serialized using JSON. So, a quick call to publish() might look like this:

```
dojox.cometd.publish(
  "/apress/firstPress",
  {
    "title":"Comet & Reverse Ajax",
    "authors": [ "Dave", "Phil" ]
  }
);
```

publish() is essentially a fire-and-forget operation. It neither returns a value nor expects a callback. If you want to see whether your message has been sent, you should subscribe to the channel that you're publishing to.

The third thing that you might want to do is to unsubscribe from a channel. The subscribe() method returns a handle object that you should pass to the unsubscribe() method. So, in a simple case, you can write this:

```
var subscription = dojox.cometd.subscribe(
  '/apress/firstPress',
  myObject,
  'handleMessage'
);

//do some comet

dojox.cometd.unsubscribe(subscription);
```

Finally, if you want to close connection to a Comet server altogether, you can call the `disconnect()` method. It takes no arguments and simply cleans up any outstanding connections and notifies the server that you are no longer interested in using its services.

So, `dojox.cometd` provides an easy-to-use client-side library for Comet. To get a full stack though, you need a working server too, so let's take a look at what's out there.

Server-Side Implementations

In the early days of Cometd, the predominant servers were written in Perl and Python. Over the course of 2007, though, the Java-based Jetty web server made its way to the front of the pack and is currently the most active Cometd server in the open-source arena. Recent versions of Jetty include a Java-based server-side implementation of the Bayeux protocol.

We already discussed Jetty's support for continuations in the previous chapter, in the context of DWR. Jetty's Bayeux implementation is defined in terms of a set of abstract base classes (the `org.mortbay.cometd` package), on top of which sits an implementation based around Jetty's continuations mechanism (the `org.mortbay.cometd.continuation` package). Most of the time that we're using Bayeux on the server, we can talk in terms of the abstract base classes but will actually be using continuations-based implementations.

To get a simple Comet demonstration running using Jetty and Bayeux, though, you don't need to write any server-side code. We'll show you how to use the Jetty Bayeux API in more detail in Chapter 7, but for our current purposes, you can use the Cometd servlet provided as part of Jetty. The class in question is

`org.mortbay.cometd.continuation.ContinuationCometdServlet`.
It's a bit of a mouthful but very simple to set up. All you need to do is assign a URL to an instance of the servlet in your web.xml file.

Because our main examples are using Grails, which generates the web.xml file for us, adding this servlet is a little bit complicated. So, before we look at Grails, let's consider the generic case. First, you would need to declare the servlet:

```
<servlet>
  <servlet-name>cometd</servlet-name>
  <servlet-class>
    org.mortbay.cometd.continuation.    \
    ContinuationCometdServlet             \
  </servlet-class>
  <load-on-startup>1</load-on-startup>
</servlet>
```

Then, you need to map a URL pattern onto the servlet:

```
<servlet-mapping>
  <servlet-name>cometd</servlet-name>
  <url-pattern>/cometd/*</url-pattern>
</servlet-mapping>
```

In this case, you're assigning our servlet to map to all URLs under the path /cometd/, which corresponds with our client-side code earlier.

To assemble a working web application from here, you simply need to add the Dojo client libraries (or point to the AOL CDN), add a page to call the `dojox.cometd` classes, and make sure the Bayeux and Cometd JAR files are on your classpath, typically by putting them in the `lib` folder of your WAR file. In the final section of this chapter, you're going to use Grails to build a working Cometd application.

Using Bayeux with Dojo and Jetty

So far, we've talked through the theory of getting up and running with Cometd and presented some sample snippets of code. To round off this chapter, you're going to build a working demonstration. We'll stick to using Grails, because in Chapter 7, we're going to rework our Magnetic Poetry example to use Cometd.

The first change that you'll need to make in your development approach is to modify the `web.xml` file. As we noted, Grails generates this for you, and, unfortunately, a standard Grails application can't alter `web.xml`. However, Grails has a mechanism for writing plug-ins, which can modify `web.xml`, and a plug-in can also be run as a stand-alone web application. So you're going to write your demonstration as a plug-in.

You'll create a new Grails plug-in project called `comet`. The project layout is mostly the same as for an ordinary Grails application, with server-side components arranged under the `grails-app` folder and client-side resources under `web-app`. In addition, there is a top-level script called `CometGrailsPlugin.groovy`, which provides you with a way in to the `web.xml` file. Within the method called `doWithWebDescriptor`, you can modify `web.xml` as a XML document. Here's your code for adding the Jetty Cometd servlet:

```
def doWithWebDescriptor = { xml ->
  def servletElement = xml.'servlet'
  servletElement[0] + {
    'servlet' {
      'servlet-name'("cometd")
      'servlet-class'(                              \
        "org.mortbay.cometd.continuation.          \
         ContinuationCometdServlet"                 \
      )
      'load on-startup'("1")
    }
  }

  def mappingElement = xml.'servlet-mapping'
  mappingElement[0] + {
    'servlet-mapping' {
      'servlet-name'("cometd")
      'url-pattern'("/cometd/*")
    }
  }
}
```

If you're not familiar with Groovy and its Builder mechanisms, the code here may look rather odd. You're working with the XML document as an object model, building up extra XML elements as a series of nested statements. First of all, you look for an existing `<servlet>` element and append the new servlet reference to the Jetty Cometd servlet after it. You then insert the `<servlet-mapping>` element in a similar way.

OK, let's get on to the code. You're going to add a laboratory page in which we can put the Cometd object through its paces. Figure 6-2 shows what this lab looks like.

Figure 6-2. The Cometd lab page

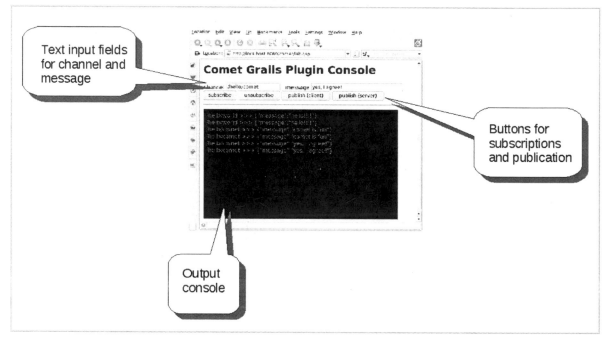

The interface is fairly basic. You've provided two text entry boxes for naming a channel and a message, respectively. Beside these, you have four buttons: the "subscribe" and "unsubscribe" buttons for your channels and two publish buttons marked as "client" and "server". You'll use the "client" button to publish using `dojox.cometd`, and we'll return to what the "server" button does later.

Underneath these controls is a black output pane, in which you're going to write messages.

When your lab page loads, you load up Dojo and the Cometd extensions and initialize the Cometd client to point at the Jetty-based server that you've set up in `web.xml`:

```
dojo.require("dojox.cometd");
dojox.cometd.init("cometd");
```

You then instantiate an object called lab that's going to contain most of your interactions with the Cometd client. First, let's look at managing subscriptions. You provide the lab object with a lookup of subscription handles and subscribe() and unsubscribe() methods:

```
var lab={
  subs:{},
  subscribe:function(channel){
    if (this.subs[channel]){
      this.output(
        "already subscribed to channel "+channel);
    }else{
      this.subs[channel]=dojox.cometd.subscribe(
        channel, this, "publishHandler"
      );
    }
  },
  publishHandler:function(msg) {
    var reply=msg.channel+" >>> "+dojo.toJson(msg.data);
    this.output(reply);
  },
  unsubscribe:function(channel){
    if (!this.subs[channel]){
      this.output("not subscribed to channel "
        +channel+" :: can't unsubscribe");
    }else{
      dojox.cometd.unsubscribe(this.subs[channel]);
    }
  },
```

The publishHandler() method is referenced as the callback to any subscription operation, regardless of channel, and simply calls an output() method to write to the console area below the buttons. Calls to dojox.cometd.subscribe() store the returned handle objects in lab.subs(), from which they can be retrieved to provide the arguments for `dojox.cometd.unsubscribe()`. The remaining core operation to perform is to publish messages:

```
publish:function(channel,msg){
  dojox.cometd.publish(channel, {"message":msg} );
},
```

`lab.publish()` is a very straightforward wrapper around `dojox.cometd.publish()`. You wrap the string entered by the user into an object with a single property called `message`. Note that one needn't be subscribed to a channel to publish on it.

The `output()` function does some routine DOM manipulation in order to display a message on the console:

```
output:function(msg){
  var output=dojo.byId('output');
  var div=document.createElement("div");
  var txt=document.createTextNode(msg);
  div.appendChild(txt);
  output.appendChild(div);
},
```

Finally, you define a `ui` object as a property of the lab, which contains bindings for the UI buttons. Mostly, these are very straightforward, simply reading values from the text fields and calling the main lab methods. In the case of the `publish()` method, though, a little more is going on, but we'll defer a discussion of that to the next section:

```
ui:{
  subscribe:function(){
    var chan=dojo.byId("channel").value;
    lab.subscribe(chan);
  },
  unsubscribe:function(){
    var chan=dojo.byId("channel").value;
    lab.unsubscribe(chan);
  },
  publish:function(clientSide){
    var chan=dojo.byId("channel").value;
    var msg=dojo.byId("message").value;
    if (clientSide){
      lab.publish(chan,msg);
    }else{
      dojo.xhrPost({
        url:"laboratory/serverEvent",
        content:{
          "channel":chan,
          "message":msg
        },
        load:function(data){
          console.output("server says "+data);
        }
      });
    }
  }
}
}
}
```

You can now run your lab page through its paces. In Figure 6-3, you've pointed two different browsers at the page and can publish and subscribe across several channels in order to create a primitive sort of chat system.

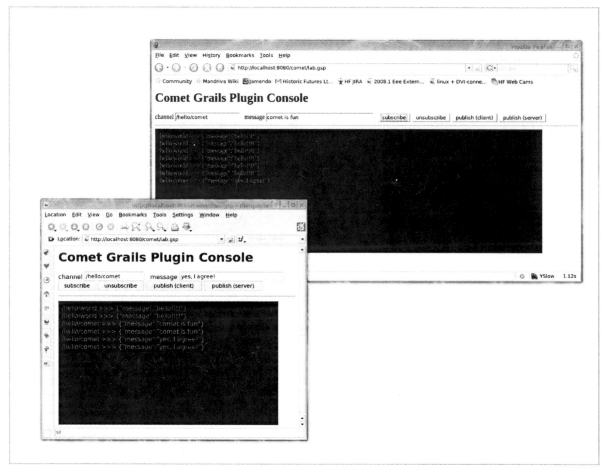

This sort of Cometd communication is trivial to set up, but do note that the capabilities of the lab as it stands only support one of the three main use cases for Comet that we outlined in Chapter 1. Let's recap those use cases in terms of the lab:

- *Allow multiple clients to collaborate by immediately seeing each other's updates*: Yes, we can support that.

- *Let the server report progress on long-running jobs*: Hmm, we can't really support that.

- *Provide a highly responsive feed that lets us monitor server-side events*: Nope, we definitely can't support that.

What's missing? Our two browsers are using the servlet as a pipe to talk directly to one another, but the server can't talk to them. If you want to be able to use Bayeux effectively, you need to be able to originate messages on both the client and the server.

Server-Side Messaging

At this point, things become a little more complex, and you'll need to look at the Comet servlet that Jetty has kindly provided us with. We won't show the code directly here—you can download it from `http://mortbay.org` if you're interested—but we'll talk through the architectural principles.

The object responsible for looking after the channels and client subscriptions to them is an instance of the Java class `dojox.cometd.Bayeux`. The Bayeux object can receive messages and assign them to clients based on channel matching but defers the HTTP transport implementation to the servlet.

As the keeper of the links between clients and channels, every servlet must have a reference to the same `Bayeux` instance; otherwise, not all clients would be able to communicate with one another reliably (see Figure 3-4). The core challenge for a server-side implementation, then, is how to enforce the singleton pattern on the `Bayeux` instance.

Figure 6-4 depicts a situation in which you have two instances of a Cometd servlet running on a server, each with a reference to its own `Bayeux` object. Clients connecting to the Cometd URL will obtain an instance randomly, so that clients A and B are connected to `Bayeux` instance 1, and client C to `Bayeux` instance 2. In spite of connecting to different `Bayeux` instances, clients A through C are all subscribed to the same channel. Other servlet types, such as servlet 2, may wish to publish to this channel. Here, servlet 2 has obtained a reference to `Bayeux` instance 1, so clients A and B will be notified, but client C will not. In the general case, multiple `Bayeux` instances will lead to random and incomplete communications, unless we adopt the overhead of somehow synchronizing the multiple instances.

Figure 6-4. Importance of enforcing a singleton pattern on the server-side Bayeux object

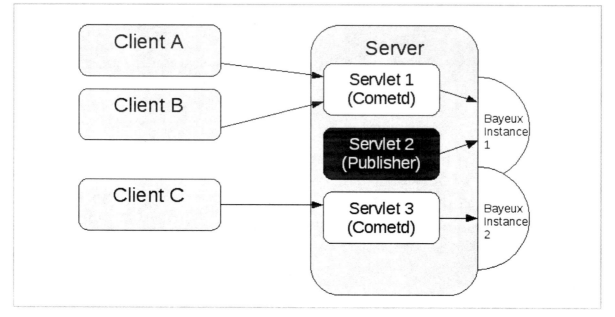

In the current implementation, the Singleton pattern is enforced by setting `Bayeux` as an attribute of the servlet context. Within the Java servlet specification, the servlet context represents the container in which the servlet is running. The Servlet specification guarantees a single servlet context for each Java Virtual Machine (JVM). So, we can guarantee a singleton `Bayeux` up to the point at which we're clustering or load-balancing across multiple servers. At that point, we'd need to adopt a more heavyweight approach, such as accessing the `Bayeux` through a networked directory such as the Java Naming and Directory Interface (JNDI) used by Enterprise Java Beans. We'd expect to see solutions of this sort as implementations of server-side Cometd mature.

OK, now let's return to your lab page. What were you doing in the `lab.ui.publish()` method? If the argument `clientSide` is set to `true`, you publish using the `dojox.cometd` client. If set to `false`—as it is when you click the mysterious "publish (server)" button—you make an ordinary Ajax request to a server-side resource. Within that resource, you're going to generate a Comet event from the server, and understanding the singleton mechanism is crucial to achieving that.

Let's take a look at the code in the Groovy controller that handles the Ajax request:

```
class LaboratoryController{
  def serverEvent={
    def chan=params['channel']
    def mess=params['message']
    def bayeux=servletContext
      .getAttribute(
         dojox.cometd.Bayeux.DOJOX_COMETD_BAYEUX
      )
    def client=bayeux.newClient("serv")
    def channel=bayeux.getChannel(chan,true)
    channel.publish(client,mess,"1234")
    render(contentType:"text/plain",content:"ok")


  }
}
```

Things start off reasonably enough, reading the request parameters to find out what message you're going to send down what channel. Then you get hold of a `Bayeux` object from the servlet context, using the key that the servlet used to place it there. (Under Grails, the variable `servletContext` is populated for you. In a plain servlet environment, you'd need to use the `servlet.getServletContext()` method).

The Java `Bayeux` object looks pretty much like the client-side one. First, you use it to create a new client. You're going to be lazy here and create a new client every time you send a message, but you could keep a reference to a client within the controller.

Next, you acquire a `Channel` object, passing in the channel name, and a `true` flag that tells the `Bayeux` to create the channel if it doesn't already exist.

In the server-side API, `publish()` is a method of the channel, and you pass in the client object and your message to it, along with a bogus client ID. The controller then returns with a simple acknowledgement. It is not responsible for passing the message on to any subscribed clients; `Bayeux` will now take care of that.

That's it then. You've built a working proof of concept using Jetty and Cometd. In the next chapter, you'll tackle the Magnetic Poetry example again using these new skills, but first, let's review what we've covered in this chapter.

Summary

Bayeux provides a very nice abstraction on top of the Comet transport, by casting the transfer of data in terms of channels, to which clients can publish and subscribe. Published messages can be free-form data structures of arbitrary complexity.

On the client-side, the Dojo Cometd client is the only horse in town and a very agreeable one at that. It provides a simple, sensible API that lets us subscribe to and unsubscribe from channels and publish messages.

On the server-side, we looked in detail at the Jetty implementations of Comet. Jetty provides an out-of-the-box servlet for enabling Dojo clients to chat to one another as well as a programmable API that allows Comet clients on the HTTP server to publish messages and subscribe to channels. This capability offers the possibility of much richer types of Comet-based architecture, as we shall see in the final chapter when we attempt to marry comet to a traditional CRUD application.

Chapter 7: Combining Comet with CRUD

Comet's event-driven architecture is new and exciting. The majority of web applications, however, are centered around a CRUD (create, read, update, and delete) architecture for managing entities.

Now that we're all fired up to use Comet, how do we integrate it into a CRUD-style application. We've already referred to CRUD in Chapter 3, in the naive implementation of the Magnetic Poetry application. Let's briefly review the typical features of a CRUD-based web application:

- Domain data is stored in a relational database

- In the business logic tier of the application, this data is represented by an object model, describing the domain in terms of entities with properties and behavior.

- Often, an "object-relational mapping" framework is used to manage the translation between object model and database table. The open-source Hibernate project (`http://www.hibernate.org`) is a popular example.

- We interact with these entities in four principal ways: creating them, reading their properties, updating their properties, and deleting them—that is, using the CRUD operations.

- A separate presentation tier of code controls how the user can interact with this domain model and defines the workflow on top of the raw domain model, following the classic Model-View-Controller (MVC) software design pattern.

Prior to Ajax, the presentation tier would typically return fully fledged HTML web pages. Although Ajax is a radical departure from the full-page–refresh approach to web development, we can still use a combination of MVC and CRUD to deliver data as JSON or XML. The Grails framework that we used to develop our magnetic poetry examples is designed around the MVC and CRUD concepts and is ideally suited for developing applications in which an object domain model is persisted to a database.

In Chapter 6, we covered the basic principles of the Bayeux specification and its Cometd implementation. Let's recap the key principles:

- All comet-based messages go over a single HTTP connection.

- Communication can be targeted between specific clients using channels.

- Clients publish messages to channels and subscribe to channels to receive the messages published by others.

- Clients can be created both on the web browser and on the server, allowing true two-way communication.

The application that we developed to demonstrate this was a simple chat room, in which several clients are transmitting transient data directly to one another, simply using the server as a conduit for their communications. Nothing gets persisted to a database. Chat rooms are the "Hello World" applications of Comet, providing a simple backdrop to demonstrating the plumbing of a particular Comet stack. As such, they are very useful, but they are also atypical of the web applications that most of us spend our time developing.

We want to round this book off with a demonstration of how the mature Comet technologies can be put to work within the more familiar context of a CRUD-based application. In this chapter, you're going to reimplement the Magnetic Poetry application using the Dojo and Jetty Cometd stack.

Revisiting Magnetic Poetry

Let's begin by reviewing the design of the Magnetic Poetry application. First of all, it's a CRUD application. The words on the magnet board are all stored in a database via an object-relational mapping (ORM) toolkit called GORM, a Grails ORM built on top of Hibernate.

Secondly, it's a collaborative application. When several users are logged in to the application, they should all receive rapid updates as to the changes in the underlying entity model made by any user.

So, each interaction with the data model on the server has to do two things:

- Update the database

- Notify other connected users of the changes

In the implementation in Chapter 3, the first goal was achieved by making conventional Ajax requests. The second goal was faked by having a separate long-lived request running on the server that polled the data model for changes. While considerably more responsive than polling over the network, this solution still put an unnecessary load on the database.

At the end of Chapter 6, you saw how you could publish to Bayeux channels from the server as well as the client. If you want to improve on the notification side of your architecture, you can make use of this facility. So, as a first cut at the design of a controller, you could consider the following strategy:

- Update the data model.

- Post a notification to a Cometd channel (from the server).

- Return an acknowledgement.

The acknowledgements in Chapter 3 consisted of small JSON objects, containing acknowledgements of deletes, updates in the version numbers that you needed to use to support our server-side polling, and so on. In short, they were fairly rich pieces of data.

Now that you have a proper event-based mechanism, you can reduce this acknowledgement to little more than a curt nod. Remember, each client connected to a Bayeux channel has a unique clientId, and all other clients subscribed to that channel will receive the published message. As you are publishing from a server-side Bayeux client, your own browser-based client (i.e., the one on the browser that initiated the request) will receive the same notification as other browser-based clients, and you can extract any rich details that you need from that.

You can support your magnetic board application by running all clients over a shared Bayeux channel and publishing updates from the server when the user posts changes. It sounds good in theory, so let's have a look at the implementation.

Client-Side Initialization Code

You'll start off by setting up the client-side infrastructure. Out of a combination of laziness and familiarity, you decide to stick with the Prototype and Scriptaculous libraries to support DOM manipulation, Ajax, drag and drop, and a number of other common tasks. In Chapter 6, we looked at the Dojo toolkit's support for cometd, for which Prototype and Scriptaculous have no equivalent.

Dojo can do everything that you're using Prototype and Scriptaculous for, but you don't really want to get caught up in a ground-up reimplementation, so let's see whether you can get the two libraries to cooperate or at least coexist peacefully. You can do so, provided you introduce them in the right order. Here's what we came up with after a little juggling:

```
<script type="text/javascript"
  src="js/dojo/dojo/dojo.js.uncompressed.js">
</script>
<script type="text/javascript"
  src="js/prototype/prototype.js"></script>
<script type="text/javascript"
  src="js/prototype/effects.js"></script>
<script type="text/javascript"
  src="js/prototype/dragdrop.js"></script>
<script type="text/javascript"
  src="js/application.js"></script>
<script type="text/javascript"
  src="js/poetry.comet.js"></script>
<script type="text/javascript">
  dojo.require("dojox.cometd");
</script>
<script type="text/javascript">
  Event.observe(
    window,
    "load",
    function(){
      initComet();
      initUI();
      initDragDrop();
    }
  );
</script>
```

Among the key points to note are that you need to introduce Dojo before
Prototype and Scriptaculous, but defer loading the Dojo cometd classes
until afterward. Also, we found that you couldn't use the Scriptaculous
wrapper script (scriptaculous.js), which normally inserts extra script
tags for you programmatically, to load the effects, drag and drop, and other
components. You must manually pull in the parts of Scriptaculous that you
need; after that, you're ready to go.

With all the third-party libraries in place, you need to initialize your own application code, which you do in the final script tag. Prior to initializing the UI or the drag-drop events, you need to set up your comet client. `initComet()` is defined in `poetry.comet.js`. Let's see what we need to do.

```
function initComet(){
  dojox.cometd.init("cometd");
  var listener={
    callback:function(msg)  {
      var data=dojo.fromJson(msg.data);
      processUpdate(data);
    }
  }
  debug("init cometd");
  var subscription=dojox.cometd.subscribe(
    "/magnetic/poetry",
    listener,
    "callback"
  );
  subscription.addCallback(
    function(){
      debug("subscribed to /magnetic/poetry ready");
      initWords();
    }
  );
}
```

First, you initialize the `dojox.cometd` subsystem itself. Then you set up a listener object containing a callback function and subscribe it to a Cometd channel. In Bayeux/Cometd applications, the use of channels is a key design decision, as it determines who can see what. Here, you want all connected clients to see the same information, so you can just decide on a hard-coded channel name. In our case, `/magnetic/poetry` seems appropriate.

Once subscribed, you call the `initWords()` function to load up the initial set of words to the client. You need to take a few extra steps here, because the request to subscribe to the Cometd channel is asynchronous. That is, `subscribe()` will return before the subscription has been fully established. The Dojo toolkit has a generic mechanism for dealing with asynchronous events, called the `Deferred` object. `Dojox.cometd.subscribe()` returns a `Deferred` object.

Think of a `Deferred` object as a promise to execute some code in the future. You can pass functions to the `Deferred` object, and they will be executed when the `Deferred` object is ready. In this particular case, the `Deferred` object will be ready when the Cometd subscription is established by our client. We won't discuss the broader topic of `Deferred` objects any further here. More information can be found at `http://api.dojotoolkit.org/jsdoc/dojo/HEAD/dojo.Deferred`.

To interact with the `Deferred` object, then, you need to add a callback to it using `addCallback()`. The callback you provide is simply an anonymous function that invokes your `initWords()` function.

Following from our previous implementation, you've defined a client-side `Word` object that reflects the basic CRUD operations. Once subscribed to the Cometd channel, you may expect to receive updates on the following events via the callback passed to `subscribe()` (as opposed to the callback passed to the `Deferred` object, which is only called once when the subscription is ready):

- Creating a new word

- Updating the position of an existing word

- Deleting a word

The callback function passed to subscribe() needs to handle all of these operations, handing them off to the appropriate CRUD handler on your client-side Word object:

```
function processUpdate(data){
  var word=Words["_"+data.id];
  if (word){
    if (!data.deleted){
      word.updateUI(data.x,data.y);
    }else{
      word.deleteUI();
    }
  }else if (!data.deleted){
    new Word(data);
  }
}
```

First, you look to see if you have an existing word. If so, you either delete it (if the deleted property is set) or update it. If no matching word already exists on the client, you create one. We'll look at how the CRUD method implementations have changed from the pre-Bayeux implementation in a minute, but first, let's look at the initialization code. After subscribing to the /magnetic/poetry channel, you called a method initWords(). What does it look like?

```
function initWords(){
  debug("initWords()");
  getWords();
}
function getWords(){
  new Ajax.Request(
    "comet/initialRead"
  );,
}
```

initWords() is just a wrapper around the getWords() function, then. getWords() makes an ordinary Ajax request—and look, you aren't even using the Dojo toolkit to do this. The request is still a `Prototype` `Ajax.Request` object, but it's greatly reduced in size compared to its counterpart from Chapter 3. Specifically, there's no callback function; you're just executing a fire-and-forget strategy, because you'll use the Cometd channels to deliver the richer acknowledgement. In order to understand how this works, you'll need to look at the server.

Server-Side Initialization Code

Let's step into the Grails code, now. You've defined a `CometController` class as before, and the URL you requested will map to the `initialRead` method, defined below:

```
def initialRead = {
  def words=Word.findAll()
  for (w in words){
    publishToChannel("/magnetic/poetry",w)
  }
  render(text:"ok")
}
```

You read all the words in the database and publish each one to the Cometd channel. You then return with a simple `ok` to say that the request succeeded. If you were being a bit more robust, you'd provide a simple client-side callback to check for the `ok`. If the check fails, you'd try again after an interval of time. But to prove the point here, let's dispense with the callback altogether. As each word is published, you'll pick it up on the client from the Comet channel, in the callback that you assigned to that role.

While we're here, let's run through our server-side mechanism for publishing objects. Here's the code for the core helper methods in your controller:

```
def bayeux=null
def bayeuxClient=null
def msgId=0

def getCometChannel(channelId){
  if (bayeux==null){
    bayeux=servletContext.getAttribute(
      dojox.cometd.Bayeux.DOJOX_COMETD_BAYEUX
    )
  }
  if (bayeuxClient==null){
    bayeuxClient=bayeux.newClient(
      "magpoetry_"+Math.floor(Math.random()*1e9)
    )
  }

  def channel=bayeux.getChannel(channelId,true)
  return channel
}

def publishToChannel(channelId,obj){
  def channel=getCometChannel(channelId)
  channel.publish(
    bayeuxClient,
    obj,
    "cometController"+msgId
  )
  msgId++
  def json=new grails.converters.JSON(obj)
  log.error("published [${msgId}] :: ${json}")
}
```

First, you define some instance members, namely a Bayeux transport
object, a client connected to that Bayeux, and a unique message ID for the
client to use when generating unique identifiers for each message that it
sends.

`getCometChannel()` returns a channel object for a given name, creating one if necessary. You can use the `ServletContext`, as in Chapter 6, to ensure that you get a singleton `Bayeux` (i.e., the same one that all other connected clients, whether on client or server) will see. You then call its `newClient()` method, this time being a bit more rigorous in ensuring that each client has a unique ID. So, all controllers will share the same `Bayeux` object, but each will have its own client, which it will reuse for every object that it publishes.

To publish an object, as in your `initialRead()` method, you call `publishToChannel()`, specifying the channel name and the object to publish, which can be any Java object.

Jetty provides a set of utilities for converting POJOs into the JSON format specified by the Bayeux protocol. By default, a Java `Object` is converted into a string by calling its `toString()` method, which even the official JavaDocs admit is a bit dubious! You can override this behavior by registering a `JSONConvertor` object against a class or interface. Several useful convertors are provided, including a reflection-based convertor for objects. When initializing your application, then, register a convertor for any classes that you wish to serialize. Here's the code for the Magnetic Poetry application, which you can find in `grails-app/conf/Bootstrap.groovy`:

```
def blackList=["class","metaClass"]
  .toArray(new String[1])
def convertor=new org.mortbay.util.ajax
  .JSONObjectConvertor(true,blackList)
org.mortbay.util.ajax.JSON
  .registerConvertor(Word.class,convertor)
```

You want to serialize instances of the `Word` domain object, so register a convertor for the `Word` class. Here, a customized `JSONObjectConvertor` has been registered by passing in a list of names of properties that you don't wish to appear in the serialized form.

So, once the appropriate convertor is set up, you can pass the Word object directly into the Channel.publish() method. You assign a unique message ID to each message that you send, incrementing the count each time.

Creating Domain Objects

As with previous implementations of the client-side code, you've defined a Word object type, and you initialize one for each word on the board. You need to create JavaScript Word objects in response to create notifications and call their update() and delete() methods too.

Here's the addWord() method, for creating a new Word:

```
function addWord(){
  var text=$F('word_text');
  var color=$F('word_color');
  var x=Math.floor(Math.random()*350);
  var y=Math.floor(Math.random()*420);
  var paramsObj={ text:text, color:color, x:x, y:y };
  new Ajax.Request(
    "comet/create",
    { parameters: paramsObj } //fire and forget
  );
}
```

Again, note that your Ajax method has no callback, as you're going to receive that via the comet channel. Here's the server-side code that handles the create operation:

```
def create = {
  def newWord=new Word(
    text:params['text'],
    color:params['color'],
    x:params['x'],
    y:params['y']
  )
  newWord.save()
  publishToChannel("/magnetic/poetry",newWord)
  render(text:"ok")
}
```

Just as in our discussion at the start of the chapter, you create a newWord object, persist it to the database, publish it to the Comet channel, and then exit with a brief acknowledgement. So, if we plot this from end to end, you can see the following sequence:

5. The user submits form to create a new word.

6. The client makes Ajax submission to the server.

7. The domain model is created and persisted.

8. The domain model published to Comet channel.

9. The clients receive notification.

10. The clients create JavaScript Word object.

11. The clients render the new word on the magnetic board.

Note that the client creating the word is notified of its existence and renders it (steps 4 through 7) in exactly the same way as all other clients subscribed to that channel. You don't need to code separately for each case. Doing things this way also ensures that the client doesn't update locally until after the data is safely stored on the server, a good rule for any Ajax application.

Updating Domain Objects

The next CRUD operation to look at is updating. When your user drags a word across the board, you fire it's update() method, defined as follows:

```
update:function(dx,dy){
    this.x=parseInt(this.x)+dx;
    this.y=parseInt(this.y)+dy;
    var params={
        id: this.id,
        x: this.x,
        y: this.y
    };
    new Ajax.Request(
        "comet/update",
        { parameters: params } //fire and forget
    );
},
```

All that has changed from previous implementations is the removal of the callback function. You'll get notified by the server of the update over the Comet channel:

```
def update = {
    def id=params['id']
    log.debug("id="+id)
    def word=Word.get(id)
    log.debug("word="+word)
    if (params['x']){ word.x=params['x'].toInteger() }
    if (params['y']){ word.y=params['y'].toInteger() }
    word.save()
    publishToChannel("/magnetic/poetry",word)
    render(text:"ok")
}
```

Again, your code can follow a simple enough process of updating the domain object and then publishing it the Comet channel. The final operation, `delete()`, also follows this pattern but with a slight twist, so let's look at that.

Deleting Domain Objects

Dragging an object to the trash can fires the `deleteMe()` operation on the JavaScript `Word` object. (Since `delete` is a reserved word in Microsoft's JScript, we had to add the cute suffix.) Once more, you can implement a fire-and-forget Ajax call on the client:

```
deleteMe:function() {
  this.pendingDeletion=true;
  new Ajax.Request(
    "comet/delete",
    { parameters: { id: this.id } }
  );
},
```

On the server, you delete the domain model using the built-in `delete()` method provided to all Grails domain entities:

```
def delete = {
  def id=params['id']
  def word=Word.get(id)
  word.delete()
  publishToChannel(
    "/magnetic/poetry",
    [id:id,deleted:true]
  )
  render(text:"ok")
}
```

Rather than publishing the deleted object, though, you want to send a token containing the flag `deleted=true` and the ID of the deleted object. The Java Comet classes let us publish any object, so we'll simply create a `HashMap` and send that. The JSON serializer will turn it into a JSON object for us, with no need to register any special convertor objects this time.

Grails is built on Groovy, and Groovy provides nice shortcuts for building up Java `Collections` objects. The square parentheses and colons simply indicate keys and values in a `HashMap`. In Java, building the `HashMap` would be a bit more verbose, but the effect would be the same.

You've now built a complete CRUD application on top of the Comet stack, using a common pattern of returning very simple acknowledgements from your Ajax requests and feeding back the richer data to all clients at once using the shared Cometd channel. That approach is ideal for building a collaborative application, which we identified in Chapter 1 as one of the three core types of "killer applications" for Comet and Reverse Ajax. We also identified two other types, namely monitoring or dashboard applications and long-term progress reports. Let's consider each of these in terms of Bayeux channels. As we suggested earlier in this chapter, a key part of designing any Cometd application is in determining how many channels we need and what we need them to do.

Monitoring and dashboard applications will, in a simple use case, share all information over a single channel and pass all updates through a central dispatch function on the client. In a more complex use case, where you wish to enforce different access levels, or integrate multiple views or modules into a single dashboard, you must create multiple channels to deliver the application.

For example, in a flight-monitoring feed at an airport, you might wish to establish two channels, `/flights/arrivals` and `/flights/departures`, to allow us to subscribe to each one individually. In a trading system handling multiple account types, you might wish to establish separate channels for different types of instruments or different levels of risk.

The third type of application is the progress report on long-running jobs. Our Magnetic Poetry application from Chapter 3 implemented an example of this, namely the magnetic pottery store through which users could order a real ceramic set of the words currently on the board and receive feedback of the manufacture process in real time. Let's take a look at implementing this feature using Cometd.

Using Cometd for Progress Reports

When you submit a job to the Magnetic Poetry bakery, you can use Cometd to report back on the progress of your job. In this case, though, there is no collaborative element to the application. You don't want other users to see updates on your batch of baked goods, and receiving updates on other users would be confusing. Hence, you would like to define a unique channel for each client.

Let's take a look at the implementation. On the client side, you have a `baker` object that handles the process, as before:

```
var baker={
  start:function(){
    this.output=$("bake_status");
    $("bake_button").hide();
    this.output.show();
    var uid=Math.floor(Math.random()*1000000000)
    this.sub=dojox.cometd.subscribe(
      "/magnetic/bakery/"+uid, this, "callback"
    );
    new Ajax.Request("comet/bake",{
      parameters: { "chanUid": uid }
    }); //fire and forget
  },
  callback:function(msg){
    var data=msg.data
    if (data=="done"){
      this.done();
    }else{
      this.output.innerHTML=data;
    }
```

```
    },
    done:function(){
      dojox.comet.unsubscribe(this.sub);
      this.output.hide();
      $("bake_button").show();
    }
  }
}
```

The `baker` has three methods. `start()` initializes the process, generating a random number to append to the channel name to which you will subscribe. Hence, you should create a personalized channel, with a name like `/magnetic/bakery/123456789`. Separating the random element out with a slash will allow you to listen to all bakery channels, if you wished to create a monitoring application of some sort, by subscribing to `/magnetic/bakery/*`. You can then kick off the baking process with a fire-and-forget Ajax call.

The `callback()` function simply extracts the text from incoming messages and displays them, unless the special token `done` is sent, in which case you call `baker.done()` to tidy up the UI and show the button again.

On the server side, you can use most of the plumbing that you already developed for the collaborative side of your application. In order to create a real fire-and-forget Ajax call, though, you'll need to spawn a separate thread in which to run your bakery process. So, the actual `bake()` method in the `Controller` is relatively small.

```
def bake={
  spawnBakerThread(params['chanUid'])
  render(text:"ok")
}
```

Most of the serious work is handed over to the `spawnBakerThread()` method, which creates a new `Thread`, which can continue to publish messages to the Cometd channel after the servlet response has completed.

```
def spawnBakerThread(channelUid){
  def channel=getCometChannel(
    "/magnetic/bakery/"+channelUid
  );
  def bakerThread=new Thread({
    writeText(channel,"firing up the oven",2000)
    def words=Word.findAll()
    for (w in words){
      writeText(channel,
        "shaping clay for '"+w.text+"'",
        1000
      )
    }
    writeText(channel,"baking...",6000)
    writeText(channel,"still baking...",4000)
    writeText(channel,"tum de tum, nice day today?",
      3000)
    writeText(channel,"still baking...",6000)
    writeText(channel,"nearly done now",2000)
    writeText(channel,"there - baked!",1000)
    writeText(channel,"cooling...",2000)
    writeText(channel,"wrapping parcel",2000)
    writeText(channel,"sending to dispatch",2000)
    writeText(channel,"done",0)
  });
  bakerThread.start();
}
```

The body of the Thread is defined in the code block passed in as an argument to the Thread constructor. Note that you need to get a reference to the Cometd channel before starting the thread, because you require the ServletContext to do so, and the Thread will be running after the servlet instance has returned to the pool. Having done this, though, you can refer to the channel in the writeText() method as follows and publish messages on it.

```
def writeText(channel,text,sleeptime){
  channel.publish(
    bayeuxClient,
    text,
    "cometController"+msgId
  )
  msgId++
  log.error("baker published [${msgId}] :: ${text}")
  if (sleeptime>0){
    Thread.currentThread().sleep(sleeptime)
  }
}
```

And that's all there is to it. You've migrated all Comet functionality in the application over to the Jetty and Cometd stack.

Additional Resources

Before we conclude our exploration of Comet, we will leave you with a few pointers toward additional resources. Comet is developing rapidly at the time of writing, and a number of new implementations of Comet, both commercial and open source, are appearing. The world of web standards also promises some interesting developments toward integrating Comet into the mainstream. We hope these sources of information will help you keep up to date in this exciting field as it continues to evolve.

Further Reading

These are the best web sites for reporting news on Comet technologies:

- *Comet Daily* (http://cometdaily.com) is a dedicated resource for the Comet community.

- *Ajaxian* (http://ajaxian.com/by/topic/comet) is a broader Ajax news site that frequently reports on Comet issues.

You might also want to check out the cometd-users dedicated mailing list at Google groups (`http://groups.google.com/group/cometd-users/`), which is frequented by both the Jetty and Dojo people, as well as your authors.

Further Implementations

In the short space of this book, we've had to limit our focus on a small number of Comet implementations, namely DWR, Jetty, and Dojo. These are, in our opinion, currently the most popular implementations and the best of breed. However, there are a number of other quality up-and-coming implementations out there, and we'd be doing you a disservice to ignore them completely. In no particular order, here are a few Comet projects and technologies to watch out for:

- *Grizzly* (`https://grizzly.dev.java.net`) is an HTTP connector in the Glassfish Java EE server designed for scalability. The project includes an implementation of the Bayeux protocol that we discussed in Chapter 7.

- *Apache Tomcat* (`http://tomcat.apache.org/tomcat-6.0doc/aio.html`) has built-in support for Comet from version 6.0 onward.

- *Kaazing Enterprise Comet* (`http://www.kaazing.com`) is a highly scalable, commercial Comet server implemented in Java.

- *Lightstreamer* (`http://www.lightstreamer.com`) is another commercial application server with support for Comet.

Emerging Standards

As with many emerging technologies, early pioneers of Comet have been concerned simply with getting the thing to work. As the technology has caught on with a broader market, discussion of standardization is inevitable, and that discussion is starting to take place. Here are two of the emerging Comet standards to keep an eye on:

- *Web sockets* (`http://www.whatwg.org/specs/web-apps/current-work/multipage/comms.html#web-sockets`) are a part of the proposed HTML 5 specification. One day, we may even see native Comet support built into the browser.

- Java Community Process JSR 315 (`http://jcp.org/en/jsr/detail?id=315`) is developing the Servlet 3.0 specification. This includes support for asynchronous nonblocking notification from the server, which would enable Comet-like architectures.

Summary

At the end of Chapter 3, we discussed a number of performance issues with the naive version of the Magnetic Poetry application that we'd developed. Let's see how your Jetty and Cometd implementation addresses these.

On the client side, we had found that most browsers will only run two concurrent HTTP requests to a given server, which resulted in blocking of ordinary Ajax requests. In this chapter, however, you've used a single Cometd connection to establish a collaborative magnetic board and report on the progress of your online bakery, with a satisfactorily low degree of coupling between the two components. All the while, you've left the second HTTP connection allowed by the browser open for fetching images and for your conventional Ajax requests.

On the server side, we suspended servlet threads but didn't release the servlet back to the pool. This limited the number of clients that we could support and increased the resource footprint of our application considerably. Here, our CRUD functionality is employing Jetty continuations to release servlets, as discussed in Chapter 5.

Because the bakery is not pausing the servlet thread but a secondary thread that references very few resources, you've also reduced the load on your servlet pool considerably.

Overall, then, this feels like a much more resilient, scalable basis on which to build our application. For those of you who like to see hard numbers, Greg Wilkins, lead developer of Jetty, has conducted some large-scale experiments on Comet scalability using Amazon's compute cloud infrastructure and has written up some of his findings at `http://cometdaily.com/2008/01/07/20000-reasons-that-comet-scales/`.

Copyright

CPSIA information can be obtained at www.ICGtesting.com
Printed in the USA
237896LV00004B/61/P